D1231328

LILA W. THOMPSON,
A WOMAN FOR ALL SEASONS

By

Donald C. Thompson

This book is a work of non-fiction. The names, events and situations are true.

ISBN: 1-4107-5319-0 (e-book)
ISBN: 1-4107-5320-4 (Paperback)

Library of Congress Control Number: 2003094230

This book is printed on acid free paper.

Printed in the United States of America
Bloomington, IN

Cover photo: Lila enjoyed dressing in the fashions of the day, by Clark, Trenton, NJ.

1stBooks - rev. 08/22/03

INTRODUCTION

How I would have loved to be on my Grandma Lila's knee as a lad, feeling her warmth and strength bestowed on me, her only grandchild. Alas, she died three years before I was born. Her life shaped three sons born to her, a foster son chosen by her, and others raised by her. I have always felt her powerful legacy and her spirit to be guiding forces in my life. She, with her husband, Joseph, was such a positive influence in so many lives in New Jersey and elsewhere, that numerous people named their daughters after her. My father, her son, and many with whom she participated in the legislature, lodges, churches and community revered the matriarch of the Thompson family.

As I found from childhood on, she was bigger than life and MY Grandma. Her greatness showed from within, in words spoken, and in her many good deeds. As she headed home from helping needy people in the Great Depression, she died tragically in a solo car crash. I was born three years later. My Grandpa Joseph, who gave me an impression of love for Grandma Lila, was filled with sadness after her death. I listened to all Dad and Grandpa shared with me about her. In the years spent researching for this book, I knew I didn't have to create a loving, caring, famous grandmother. The hours spent reading newspapers and public records, and interviewing living witnesses proved she was all that and more.

Dad changed his attitude toward me after his wife, my stepmother, Ruth died in May 1978. For no reason except his grief at Ruth's loss, he limited and withheld information from me about his mother. As I worked through my anger toward him, I found additional printed articles in newspapers, N.J. legislative records, interviews, letters, and many tributes to Lila, which strengthened and corrected his information. Therefore, his withdrawal from sharing data on Lila actually strengthened this book. Throughout my life, I knew I was and am special, too, from all she was and did.

The title for this book was decided years ago when I first gathered materials to write about Lila. It is an analogy to Sir Thomas More, 1478-1535, *A Man For All Seasons* and chief advisor to England's King Henry VIII, who refused to endorse Henry's divorce of his first wife. More was executed for maintaining his integrity and canonized in 1935. I decided to write about Lila after I completed my first book, *The Application of Paulo Freire to U.S. Adult Education.* It analyzes Paulo Freire, the Brazilian educator, his approach known throughout much of the world, and applies it to the USA, based on my research in California and Arizona.

I appreciate all members of my family and friends, who have contributed to this book, especially Kenneth Potter and Mildred Potter Ivins, Lila's surviving nephew and niece, and particularly my wife, Jane Riley Thompson, my editor and co-researcher, for the countless years she has devoted to making this book outstanding. Many thanks to Professor George E. Tuttle, our secondary editor.

I dedicate this book to my children, Joel Kelley, James Dale & Donald Ross Thompson and Tara Denise Sunnarborg, Lila's great grandchildren. They continually inspire me.

Lila lived the words of James, "Show me your faith apart from your works and I by my works will show you my faith."[1] Lila is emulated and eulogized to this day in the twenty-first century. I offer this book so that her example may inspire others into service for and with all people.

Donald C. Thompson

---

[1] By the brother of Jesus, James 2:18b, *The New Testament In Four Versions, Revised Standard,* Christianity Today, Washington, DC, 1965, p.724

TABLE OF CONTENTS

PROLOGUE

LILA W. THOMPSON was born LILA WORRELL ROBBINS, March 9, 1875 and died April 3, 1933. In 1923 she was the first woman elected to the New Jersey (NJ) state legislature from a county (Ocean) where there was only one representative. She chaired and served on several committees in the General Assembly (Assembly) 1924-25, with her foci on building much needed paved roads, patriotic expressions, providing World War I (WWI) veterans' pensions and services for all people in need. Lila achieved many firsts.

In her last eight years, she gave herself completely to the needs of all people as the Great Depression struck South Jersey. Returning home to New Egypt one night, completely exhausted from her efforts as first Director of the Ocean County Old Age Pension Relief Bureau (Welfare Department) she apparently fell asleep at the wheel, and died in a tragic auto crash. Her funeral was the largest in Ocean County up to that time, showing the people's gratitude for Lila.

CHAPTER ONE

LILA'S BACKGROUND

"Then the seven years of plenty that had been in the land of Egypt came to an end. The seven years of famine began to come as Joseph had said. There was famine in every country, but there was bread to be had in Egypt." (Genesis 41:53-55)[1]

Chapter One examines the historical background and naming of her hometown, New Egypt, New Jersey; the agrarian nature, the pine barrens and other characteristics of central NJ in the early twentieth century; preceded by changes and events at the end of the nineteenth century in USA.

THE LOCAL SETTING

Lila was born in New Egypt, Plumsted Township, the northwestern corner of Ocean County in the center of New Jersey, seven miles from Ft. Dix (now) and sixteen miles from Trenton. Burlington County is on the west and Monmouth County on the north of Ocean County. Farms such as the Charles Atkinson (now David Atkinson) property outside New Egypt had land in all three counties.

Many years ago a man named Waln, for a barrel of cider and a few beads, purchased the community from the Lahwah Indians. New Egypt began as two separate settlements in the early 1700's, Snuff Mill and Timmons Mills. Snuff Mill was named for its snuff, a preparation of pulverized, cured tobacco to be inhaled through the nostrils, chewed or placed against the gums, today called smokeless tobacco. In contrast, grist was grain for grinding into products like flour, meal or grain by-products, such as corn seed and stock feeds, as processed in Timmons Mills. The grist mill stood near the center of

---

[1] *The Jerusalem Bible*, p.48

New Egypt until mid-way into the twentieth century. Snuff Mill thrived, but was overshadowed by Timmons Mills to the southwest.

THE NAME "NEW EGYPT"

Variations of the naming of the town exist in differing accounts of the *New Egypt Press* in "Way Back When" columns over many years and in Dorothy S. Mount's *A Story of New Egypt and Plumsted Township*, 1979. The naming described here is from my New Egypt Grammar School education, 1946-50, under Mrs. Dorothy Mount, Mrs. Allen, Mrs. Horner, and Miss Myrtle Moore and the Moore Brothers *History of New Egypt in the Pines*, 1911.[2]

About 1770, during a period of plenty, traditionally seven years (reported in the *New Egypt Press* to be two years), Ezekiel Timmons, a grist mill operator wisely stocked his storage bins to capacity with seed corn and grains. Traditionally seven years followed (reported in the *New Egypt Press* to be more than two years) of failed crops when people and livestock suffered and struggled and were weak with hunger. Farmers tried planting new acreage after the first failure, but the scalding sun the following summer also withered their crops and their hopes. This was when Timmons visionary planning with a large stock in the mill of extra corn, especially seed, was salvation. Farmers and merchants from near and far were compelled to travel to Timmons Mills for grain during the famine. This little piece of country, Timmons Mills and Snuff Mill, was dubbed Egypt, then New Egypt and it flourished. It was the only place farmers could get seed corn, other grain, and grain products. For the same reason that the Hebrews came to the country of Egypt in ancient times in the story of Joseph, who received his brothers in their quest for grain, hungry farmers came to New Egypt. (Genesis 41:46-43:15)[3]

---

[2] *History of New Egypt in the Pines*, New Egypt, Ocean County, New Jersey, Moore Brothers, 1911

[3] *The Jerusalem Bible*, p.48-50; "New Egypt History to be Relived" by Shelly O'Brien; *New Egypt (NE) Press*, May 28, 1986

The New Egypt mills continued to provide life. For example, one of the worst years for crops was 1816. "The year 1816 was known throughout the U.S. as the 'year without summer.' January was so mild that most people would have let their furnaces go out if they possessed any. February was only occasionally colder. March and April coaxed the buds and flowers out. May was a winter month, with ice and snow. By the end of May everything perishable had been stripped from trees. June was as cold as May. Both snow and ice were common throughout the month all over the Corn Belt and after having planted, [farmers] threw up their hands. Snow fell ten inches deep in Vermont. The following winter was the hardest: one had to have a stockade around one's smoke-house [and summer brought extreme heat and drought]. New Egypt was the only place farmers could come to get seed corn." (Jacob Compton, then almost 90 years old, quoting his father and the *Philadelphia Record*)[4]

New Egypt continued as the official name except for a brief lapse in 1869-1871, when the name was changed to Oakford.

EARLY TWENTIETH CENTURY CONDITIONS

Analogous to the naming of her hometown, New Egypt, Lila W. Thompson provided for the needs of people in Ocean County and NJ in times of great struggle, particularly 1923-1933. Her priorities included construction of paved roads, old age benefits for veterans' and other elders', and particularly ending severe food shortages and economic hardships for all of Ocean County after 1929. [5]

During Lila's lifetime, (1875-1933) Ocean County was rural thinly populated farm country with the bulk of land in primeval pine

---

[4] *NE Press*, May 28, 1915, reprinted May 15, 1980 and Dorothy S. Mount, *The Story of New Egypt and Plumsted Township*, 1979, p.1

[5] Mount, Dorothy S. *The Story of New Egypt and Plumsted Township*, 1979, p.1. Later Coperthwaite Kimmons was the visionary mill owner of Timmons Mills, who provided seed and grain to needy farmers and others. This is the source of some calling the town Kimmons Mills.

woods, called the Pine Barrens, dotted with cedar lakes (brown water from cedars), cranberry bogs, blueberry patches, natural habitats for migrating birds, and industrious people, called Pineys, surviving on the land. In the post-revolutionary war period, these descendents of smugglers and privateers, or Tories, developed new industries in the Pine Barrens south and east of New Egypt. Lumber, iron, cordwood, charcoal, sea and land transportation of Pinelands' products were backbones of their survival in the pines through the nineteenth century. Despite their industrious survival and contributions to the development of the USA, Pineys were branded as illiterate and immoral in the early twentieth century. This stereotype increased with the Pine Barrens becoming a center of the bootlegging industry during Prohibition.[6]

On the eve of WWI, New Egypt was the principal station of the Pemberton and Hightstown Railroad and the Union Transportation Company, to the east and north of the pinelands, connecting the dairies and most fertile farming areas for fruits and vegetables to the markets, and fostering telegraph and telephone communication. The Atlantic Ocean on the east of the county and state along with Oakford Lake/Crosswicks Creek in New Egypt, greatly flavored the area by attracting summer vacationers to New Egypt, along with the making and selling of crafts. The forms of summer tourism took root with twenty-five hotels and boarding houses that increased the summer population by several thousand. There were many stores and small factories. Electricity lighted the streets and a 260 feet deep pure artesian well, dug in 1911, provided the community with water. The Pineys, later vindicated by history, were not part of New Egypt's promotional material.

Neither was Camp Dix, later Fort Dix, which polluted Oakford Lake/ Crosswicks Creek beginning during WWI, seriously reducing tourism. Still, New Egypt was the hub of improving highway transportation to the shore until late in the 1930's when Routes 70 &

---

[6] Miller, Pauline S., *Ocean County: Four Centuries in the Making*, p.153-157

38 were constructed and bypassed New Egypt from Philadelphia and Trenton to the shore.[7]

THE NATIONAL SETTING

Nationally, USA became an imperial power in 1898 in the Spanish American War. Republican President Theodore Roosevelt broke new ground for political reform. USA added to its power in WWI, while autos, airplanes, trains, income taxes, telephones, transcontinental cable, continually growing industry, urbanization, and the use of electric power and lights changed the face of America forever from its rural farm center at Lila's birth in 1875. [8]

Livelihood on the farm depended on the weather and the prices. Farm life was twenty-four hours a day, seven days a week hard work, even drudgery. Imagine the daily loss of life nearing the end of the 19th century: half the children born did not reach adulthood. There were other smaller tragedies without modern medicine to aid animals or sick people. Frequent fires, storms and famines devastated farms in NJ and the country. But there was a heartiness, an endurance, and, indeed, a faith that with God's help, all was possible. There was a reality of being grounded in the earth and caring for the environment, as well as mutual interdependence, which meant survival together, or not at all! Seldom did a child rise above the provincial confines of rural New Jersey to blaze new creative paths. Lila was one of the trailblazers.[9]

---

[7] *Exploring the History of Southern Ocean County*, Long Beach Island, NJ Tourist Publication, 1997; *History of New Egypt in the Pines, 1911*

[8] Langer, Wm. L., ed., *An Encyclopedia of World History*, Houghton Mifflin, Harvard, 1952, p.787-88

[9] New Egypt area, one of the largest farm producing areas in Ocean county, Miller, Pauline S., *Ocean County, Four Centuries in the Making*, Ocean County Cultural & Heritage Commission, Toms River, NJ, 2000, p.211

Donald C. Thompson

CHAPTER TWO

THEIR GLORIES WILL NOT FADE

"Do not displace the ancient landmark set by your ancestors." (Proverbs 22:28)[8]

Chapter Two highlights the Robbins and Hankins families' histories, Lila's parents, and the strong character instilled in her.

THE ROBBINS FAMILY AND FARM

FATHER THEODORE ROBBINS (1832-1917)

Lila's father, Theodore, was a New Egypt farmer and blacksmith. The location of the Robbins, Sr. farm, later called the Wikswo farm, is on a hill on the north side of Archertown Road. Originally built in 1776 by Thomas Shinn, the farm is just east of the former Vernon Dancer Farm- a "bed and breakfast" now. The Robbins sharecropped the nearby Balderson farm on a 40-60 basis, while operating their own farm. The clay from the Robbins farm hill was used to make bricks at a brickyard operated by James Hiland. There were several tenant houses for the workmen at the brickyard. This was the farm where Theodore Robbins, Sr. lived and grandson Kenneth Potter was born Nov. 28, 1904. In addition to the many farm and brickyard tasks, Theodore, Sr. was a busy farrier, replacing the shoes on most of the horses in the area. His blacksmith shop was downtown at 16 Front Street beside the Presbyterian Church.[9]

The Robbins' ancestors were English royalty, entitled to a coat of arms. Daniel was the first Robbins to move to the British colonies in New England. Because of religious oppression (The Robbins were

---

[8] *The Jerusalem Bible*, Doubleday, Garden City, NY, 1968, p. 840
[9] Mount, Dorothy, p. 9, 21

Quakers.) he came with the Boones and the Lincolns in 1670 to the Woodbridge, NJ area. The Robbins family was among the original settlers and became a prominent pioneer family.[9]

The British ruling class, restoring Charles II to the throne in 1660, was concerned about other countries' claims to the colonies, because the Dutch were moving into New Netherlands, Manhattan and what later became New Jersey, while the Swedes were moving into what became Delaware and Maryland. So Daniel Robbins was granted 173 acres of land by a British lord and was a town officer-tax collector, constable, etc. He and his wife, Hope, raised nine children. Their descendants, starting in 1695, were among the first settlers of Monmouth County, NJ. Included were the Lincoln and Boone (later Daniel, legendary frontiersman) families, before they moved to Kentucky. Deborah Lincoln, President Abraham Lincoln's aunt, is buried in the Robbins cemetery in Allentown, NJ. The Robbins family remained in Monmouth County and Ocean County.[10]

During the Revolutionary War, several Robbins' men served in the militia: Isaac, Jesse, John, and Joseph. Continental Army veterans were Thomas and William. In the March 1782 British attack on the Toms River, NJ Blockhouse, defender Moses Robbins was wounded and became a hero. After the British burned the town, Moses was the first to rebuild. Earlier, Elijah was the first Toms River Postmaster and provided the land on which the Blockhouse had been built.[11]

In the nineteenth century, Johnson Robbins and Elmira Davis were the parents of Theodore Robbins. He was a Quaker, but there were no Friends' meetings nearby, so the family attended the New Egypt Presbyterian Church. Theodore was a strong husky man, a blacksmith and a farmer. In those days young men wrestled to see who could throw and pin the other down. One time some gamblers from Trenton brought two young men to wrestle Theodore. He was

---

[10] Claude Thompson *Interviews*, 1951, 1976, Kenneth Potter *Interview*, 1999, & Robbins records; Robbins cemetery in Allentown had a tower.

[11] Heston, Alfred, *History of South Jersey*, 1923, p. 53-54

ready. He wrestled the two of them and threw and pinned them both. The Trenton gamblers lost their money that day. [12]

Father Theodore lived to be eighty-five and set a deep spiritual and firm moral basis, with a strong work ethic and a propensity for service for all his children. He would have lived longer had a chair not broken under him when he was repairing a curtain rod. He fell and struck his head. Five days later he had a stroke and never regained consciousness. The cause of death was recorded as apoplexy (stroke today). Widely respected in the area, he lived long enough (May 19, 1917) to be very proud of Lila's early accomplishments. [13]

THE HANKINS FAMILY

MOTHER LYDIA A. HANKINS ROBBINS (1837-1906)

Lila's mother was a thin, but not a tall woman, and a wonderful woman. She was a Hankins, from a good old-line English family who came to the British colonies years earlier. Private (NJ) Zechariah Hankins, Sr. died a hero during the Revolutionary War, (DAR Patriot Index, p.301). Henry H. Hankins, born Dec. 26, 1842, served in the Grand Army of the Republic (GAR), fought in twenty-seven battles in the Civil War and was wounded five times. He spent seven and one-half months in Libby Prison, Richmond, VA, for officers and enlisted men, in miserable, unsanitary conditions among a sweltering mass of humanity, where the majority of prisoners did not survive. Miraculously, Henry survived and was present at General Lee's surrender at Appomattox, VA. After the war, he was a house and bridge builder, and a professional hog killer, slaying over 74,250 hogs, a New Jersey record. [14]

---

[12] Claude Thompson *Interview* with Linda Fote, 1983
[13] Ibid
[14] Ocean County Historical Society, Toms River, Hankins File, and Internet, Libby Prison; Linda Fote *Interview*

David C. Hankins, 1834-1907, GAR, Civil War veteran from 1861, was Lydia's brother. James Hankins had his moment of fame in the early days of airmail, when he took the first sack of Pemberton, NJ airmail to an awaiting airplane. [15]

The philosophy of the nineteenth century was to have as many children as possible for farming, wars, and caring for aging parents. Twelve of the sixteen children of Theodore and Lydia Robbins grew to adulthood, a very good average for those born between 1855 and 1882.

Lydia was one of ten children of James Benson Hankins (1807-1853) and Rejoice Chamberlain (1808-1830); three were stillborn. Lydia bore sixteen children, four died early in life. While the remaining children were growing up, Mother Lydia had the bulk of the household chores and the responsibility for nurturing, as well as daily farm tasks, such as cleaning eggs, preparing foods for preserving, preparing the meals, doing laundry on a scrub board, etc. As the children grew, they took on their share of the tasks with Mother Lydia supervising. She set the example, as did her husband, of spirituality, hard work, service, honesty and integrity for all their children. She was a woman of great ambitions, especially for the children. Lila came from that hearty stock.[16]

Lydia used the light of day and an oil lamp to go into the cellar to work. One day as she started her tasks, she spotted a skunk, which at first shied away from the light. Showing her 'spunk,' she used the oil lamp to attract the skunk. Lydia skillfully lured the intruder around the cellar and into an old barrel. This was no easy task for a strong man, let alone a thin, not physically strong woman. When she told her non-swearing husband she had caught a skunk, "The hell you say," was his reply. He investigated and to his surprise he found the skunk trapped in the barrel. [17]

---

[15] Ocean County Historical Society, Hankins File

[16] Claude Thompson *Interview* with Linda Fote, Feb. 1983 and *NE Press*, Nov.11, 1971

[17] Dad's favorite story about Grandma Lydia, told to me from childhood

After a few days' illness, Lydia, sixty-nine, died of pneumonia in New Egypt on Nov. 5, 1906, the same day as Irene DeCou's birth, later Claude Thompson's wife. [18]

---

[18] Ibid and Lila W. Thompson's *Family Bible,* Records Section.

Donald C. Thompson

CHAPTER THREE

THE LILA STORY; THE BEGINNING

"Jesus said, 'Let the children come unto me, and do not hinder them; for to such belongs the kingdom of heaven.'" (Matt. 13:14 RSV)[19]

Chapter Three addresses Lila's birth and early life, her siblings and some of their histories and offspring, as well as early testimonies to Lila.

LILA

Lila Worrell Robbins was born Tuesday, March 9, 1875, one of sixteen children, including one set of twins, born from 1855 to 1882, on the Robbins farm east of New Egypt. She was the twelfth child of sixteen children born (included in the birth records of Ocean County/Plumsted Township and the reports of family) to Theodore and Lydia Hankins Robbins; twelve survived to adult life. Theirs was a respected farm family, emphasizing God, responsibility, honesty and integrity.[20]

LILA'S SIBLINGS

Theodore and Lydia had a large family. According to Plumsted Township birth records, the first-born was a son, Johnson - 1855, named for Theodore's father; then Elmira, -1856, named for Theodore's mother; Elmina—1859 (one was called El or Ella); John H. (Johnny)—1860; William (Will)—1862; Anna—1864; Charles—

---

[19] *The New Testament in Four Versions; Revised Standard,* p.38
[20] *Plumsted Township / Ocean County Birth Records*, 1848-1923, researched by Elizabeth Ann Grant, May 1989

1866; Theodore (Dory)—1868; Estella ('Stell')—1871; Samuel—1872; Carrie—1873; Lila—1875; the twins, Leon & Lewis, 1880; and the last born, Lydia, -1882, named for her mother. No birth date was recorded for Mary. The twins died in infancy.[21]

Anna, a trained nurse, married Francis R. Hope and bore a set of twins. I, Lila's grandson, am the father of twins, Dale and Ross Thompson born Aug. 5, 1964. Lila's adult life and contributions are matters of public record; unfortunately the Plumsted Township and Ocean County birth and wedding records of Robbins family members were not complete in the 1800's. Most of the family members are buried in Jacobstown Schoolhouse, Methodist and Baptist cemeteries. Johnny was the only child who resided outside of New Jersey, moving to California at age nineteen. Johnny never returned. I, without knowing it, followed in Johnny's footsteps eighty-seven years later when I moved to Los Angeles.[22]

Charles W. Robbins married Carrie Glover, November 20, 1888. In 1908, Charles W. Robbins Cash Grocery and Meat Market, New Egypt, sold Choice Roast Beef for fourteen cents a pound and Sirloin Steak for eighteen cents a pound, listed among his Saturday specials.[23] In 1906, Charles bought a six horsepower steam engine to run the sausage-grinding machine.[22] In November 1929, the Board of Managers of the Eastern Star Home for the Aged at Bernardsville, NJ appointed Charles, sixty-three, as Superintendent. Lila, a Board member, made sure that the caring leadership of her brother guided the Home through the Great Depression; she had been instrumental in securing and adapting the castle-like structure as a retirement home. [24]

Theodore, Jr. (Dory) lived and farmed in Hornerstown, NJ.[25] He and his wife struggled with the disease of alcoholism. The rest of

---

[21] *Plumsted Township / Ocean County Birth Records*, 1848-1923, Researched by Elizabeth Ann Grant, 1989
[22] Claude Thompson *Interview* and my personal reflections
[23] *NE Press*, Nov. 8, 1908
[22] *NE Press*, Dec. 9, 1906
[24] *NE Press*, Nov. 29, 1929; F. Elwood Perkins letter, Oct. 18, 1977
[25] *NE Press*, Nov. 11, 1906

the family helped raise Dory's children. Another brother, Samuel Robbins, married Matilda Blum, April 12, 1899, and they farmed nearby.[26]

Will Robbins was the patriarch of the Pine View Boarding House and Farm of one hundred acres on Brindletown Road from 1899 to 1960. He lived to be ninety-eight, was a seventy-five year Masonic Lodge member, and was known for reciting poetry until the end of his life. After a full workday, he loved to listen to the radio news with the sound turned high. Will's son Theodore J. and wife, Sarah L. Emery, married June 14, 1915, and operated the Pine View Farm from World War II until Feb. 6, 1976 when fire leveled the historic farm and boarding house buildings. They were historic because this was the traditional site of the original mansion house built for the Proprietor, Clement Plumstead, in the late 1600's. Pine View Farm lodged many summer visitors until wastes from Camp Dix polluted Crosswicks Creek during World War I. Sadly, many Robbins' historic documents, records and pictures were destroyed when the house and farm buildings burned. Theodore and Sarah spent their last years with their adopted daughter and her family in Forked River.[27]

I grew up in New Egypt, 1936-1954, and remember Will Robbins, the farm and its nutritious dairy products. My father, Claude, always gave credit to the farm and its fresh dairy products and produce for helping me grow tall, having shot up seven inches between seventh and eighth grades. I also remember Lydia A. Robbins, the youngest, who married George H. Tripple, November 29, 1900. They lived in Camden and later Ocean City, NJ, where I met them. She was the last of the Robbins siblings to die, at age ninety-one, in 1973. She maintained an active correspondence with our family through the 1960's. [28]

---

[26] *Plumsted Township / Ocean County Vital Statistics* (Marriages), 1848-1923

[27] Mount, Dorothy S., *A Story of New Egypt and Plumsted Township* p. 64-65

[28] *NE Press*, Nov. 11, 1971 and Mar. 11, 1971

SOWING THE SEEDS

Without early formal training, Lila and her sister Estella became self-trained elocutionists, and enhanced their skills at the Academy. They were known in the area for their well-developed speeches. This contributed greatly to Lila's and Estella's success and positive self-esteem. Estella married George H. Potter, May 12, 1892, one year after Lila married, and was the mother of two well known and life long residents of New Egypt: Mildred Potter, who married Ted Ivins, and Kenneth (Kenny) Potter, who was born Nov. 28, 1904 on his grandparents Robbins' farm. He married Mrs. Eva Hopkins Horner on July 4, 1930. They observed their seventy-second wedding anniversary in 2002, while residing with her son Charles and Elizabeth Horner across the road from where Kenny was born. I visited with them at the Horner's house in June 2002.[29]

As a child, Kenny was allowed to drive a team of horses on the neighboring farm of an Irishman, John Meany. Asked to back up the horses, the young lad cried, "I can't!" Meany responded, "You'll never know if you don't try!" Kenny tried and succeeded. From that moment on, Meany's response became Kenny's lifetime motto. This is the same spirit in which Lila operated. [30]

Kenny continued with a legend about his well-known ancestor, Thomas Potter, a farmer and fisherman at Cranberry Inlet in Good Luck, NJ. George H. Potter, Kenny's father came from that part of Ocean County. Thomas studied his Bible and believed not in hell, but in a Loving God with salvation for everyone. This was the Universalist belief that had not yet reached the New World. Without having a preacher, Thomas built a church on his farm in 1766, the Thomas Potter Meeting House. He believed a preacher would come and occupy the pulpit. In 1770 a British ship on its way to Philadelphia was blown off course into Cranberry Inlet. Passengers went ashore and John Murray, born December 10, 1741 in England,

---

[29] Kenneth Potter *Interviews*, 1999, 2002
[30] Kenneth Potter *Interviews*, 1999, 2001

was directed to the Potter farm. Kenny claimed that his ancestor, Thomas, was a generous man and offered food and lodging to John Murray. Thomas believed Murray was the preacher he'd been waiting for. Murray had been a Methodist minister in England where he read and heard a Universalist preacher and converted with his wife to Universalism. Unfortunately his wife and child both died and the cost of care put Murray into debtor's prison. A brother bailed him out and sent him to the New World. A bitter Murray said he would never preach again. Thomas revealed that he felt Murray was his preacher. Murray refused, expecting the wind to change and the ship to sail. If it didn't change, he promised to preach. The wind did not change and the ship did not sail. Murray kept his promise and preached the Universalist message, the first clergy delivered sermon at Thomas Potter's church. Later Murray preached all along the Eastern Seaboard.[31]

I was in awe as Kenny related this tale, as I had often used this very story as a sermon illustration of faith and hope. In fact, I had visited Murray Grove, now a Unitarian Universalist camp and conference center, the Good Luck cemetery and Thomas Potter church (present structure built 1841). The plaque at the church reads: "Near this spot first met Thomas Potter the Prophet and John Murray the Apostle of Universalism. Sept. 30, 1770 Murray first preached in America. The wilderness and the solitary place was glad for them." Until now, I had not made the connection between Mildred and Kenny and their famous ancestor. I appreciate their willingness to share their stories. [32]

Their mother, Estella Potter, died of pneumonia at age forty-eight, in 1920, leaving Kenneth, fifteen; Mildred, eleven; and their father, George Potter, to survive on their own.[33] For thirty-nine years (1937-1976) Kenny was a member of the Plumsted Township Committee, the governing body of New Egypt, being elected thirteen

---

[31] *Interview* June 26, 2002 with Kenneth Potter; Plaque and Museum at Murray Grove, Unitarian Universalist Camp and Conference Center, Good Luck, NJ.

[32] Ibid

[33] *NE Press*," 1920 and Dec. 1976; Kenneth Potter *Interview*, 1999

times, serving most of those years as mayor, and leaving a legacy of efficient planning and operation of the township without a local municipal tax. He never lacked a positive story about Aunt Lila.

Carrie Robbins married Oliver P. Eldridge; they were parents of five small children including Russell, when she died from consumption at age thirty-two. Ella (Elmira or Elmina) married Mr. McKoy of Cream Ridge; their daughter was Mae Hebner; her daughter was Jean. Mary Robbins married Jake McKaig and had a son, Charles.

EARLY ENDORSEMENT

Lila was never at odds with any of her sisters, and especially close with Estella. Lila sometimes "butted heads a little bit with some of her brothers." From my experience, then surviving siblings, Charles and Will Robbins and Lydia Robbins Tripple were extremely proud of Lila and her achievements.[34]

A small autograph book dated 1886 was found amongst the Lila memorabilia; Lila was ten years old.

Dear Daughter,
    Remember thy Creator in the days of thy youth.
                Your father, Theodore Robbins

My little friend,
    May you improve each moment of time.
                Your teacher, S. C. Lamb

Life is but a summer day, if we choose to make it.
Sunshine has been freely given; freely let us take it.
                J.M. Fischer

---

[34] Kenny Potter and Claude Thompson *Interviews*

Your album is a golden spot in which to write forget-me-not.

Your Friend, Joseph W. Fischer

Dear Lila,

A thought is a little thing. Of good or of ill a seed; That may joy and gladness bring, Or be but a useless weed; Then cherish the little seeds, Of thoughts that are good and pure; That blossom in loving deeds, And ripen in harvest assure.

The advice of your sister Anna, Jan. 6, 1886

Dear Sister,

Love me little; Love me long. Love me 'til I'm dead and gone.

Sister Estella, Jan. 4, 1886

Dear Sister,

Always remember to say your prayers and mind your p's and q's,

Climbing up the Golden stairs,

Your sister Carrie

Lila,

May your virtues ever shine,

Like a bobtail chicken in a watermelon rind.

Your brother, Charles Robbins

Lila,

I wish you a husband both gallant and true,

Proud of himself, but prouder of you.

Your ever friend, Anna Rahilly[35]

---

[35] *An Autograph Book*, Jan. 1886; one of the few remaining memorabilia of Lila W. Robbins Thompson; Two other autograph books from 1880's express similar tributes to her.

Lila was also blessed as her parents and siblings were grateful for Lila and supported her in her endeavors. She was loved and celebrated by each. Her father lived long enough to witness many of her accomplishments. Reports from those growing up in such large families point out that it was important to establish one's mark beyond the family. With her appealing personality and caring for others, Lila fulfilled her potential and established herself in beneficent and remarkable ways.

Her friend, Anna, was psychic in her wishes for Lila in the future. First we will explore Lila's background on the farm and at the Academy.

CHAPTER FOUR

COOPERATING IN COMMUNITY

"All who believed were together and had all things in common; and they sold their possessions and goods and distributed them to all, as any had need." (Acts 2:44-45, RSV)[36]

Chapter Four attests to Lila's growing up in the extreme hardship of farm life in the late nineteenth century. The courtship, marriage, family and community life of Lila and Joseph M. Thompson and the twentieth century factors preparing Lila's way to the Assembly highlight this chapter.

BRED IN THE BONE

Step back to 1875 and examine the farm life of South Jersey that birthed and bred Lila. Life was extremely rugged on the farm close to the Pine Barrens. The survival rate of children was low. There were sixteen children in the Robbins family with twelve surviving into adult life. This was a high survival percentage. On average in the middle to late 1800's, half the children died in birth or from childhood diseases. Lila was one of the youngest children; it was five years after her birth before the twins were born and they did not live long, so she had seven years when she was the bright and shining youngest child, until sister Lydia was born. Lila did her share of inside and outside farm tasks, including milking cows, carrying the milk, dumping it in the tub, than pouring the milk into large cans. She always brought a special lively positive spirit to all her work.

In addition, survival on the farm depended on the weather, the yield from crops, the health of the animals, and the prices of both. It was hard and constant work, even drudgery. As a child growing up in

---

[36] *The New Testament in Four Versions, Revised Standard,* p.347

town, I couldn't understand why my aunt, uncle and cousin on the farm could not take a week to come with us to the Jersey Shore. Why? They had the daily tasks of animals to feed and crops to care for, of milking the cows and gathering the eggs, readying farm products for market, not to mention the difficult household tasks. From early ages, farm children were very much workers with the adults. Lila gave special care to the horses and rode around the entire farm on horseback or in the buckboard every opportunity she had.[37]

The daily loss of life and lesser tragedies occurred frequently. In 2001, the Public Broadcasting System sent three modern families to Montana to homestead as the pioneers did in 1883. There was no electricity, radio, television, airplanes, plastics, phonograph, cars, computers, indoor plumbing, nor most of the things we take for granted now. Food had to be prepared completely, cooking over an open fire or wood stove. Cows were milked outside in the snow. Houses had to be built from cutting the trees down and fitting them together into log cabins. In the early stages some in the families could hardly wait to get back to today's living conditions and were sorry they had committed to the project. Watching this PBS series helped me understand the hardships endured more than a century ago in Lila's family. [38]

On the other hand, PBS also showed that within the homesteading families they had closeness with each other not experienced in modern life. Parents got to know each other and their children, and children came to closeness with their parents through their successes in surviving together. The difficulty added to the intensity of the experience. The cooperation in working together was the key. Each person developed basic skills they didn't know they possessed. For example, a daughter found special skill in caring for the animals that helped their milk and egg production increase and she even nurtured them from sickness to health. Further, the three families

---

[37] Saunders, Ernest W. *Searching The Scriptures: A History of Biblical Literature, 1880-1980*, Scholars Press, Chico, Cal., 1982, p. 3-23 and my careful observation and participation as a worker on farms growing up.

[38] *Frontier House*, PBS, April 29 & 30, 2002; History Major, Dickinson College.

often had difficulty sharing their supplies and resources with each other, tending to hoard things for themselves. When they did share work and resources they found that all benefited.

Lila learned these lessons of cooperation and survival on the Robbins farm and lived them throughout her adult life.[39] Inside the South Jersey farmhouse kitchen there was a wood stove on a concrete slab for cooking and heat. Boiled water from large kettles was poured into copper tubs used for doing the laundry. A scrub board on which to wash and hand scrub the soiled laundry was a part of that difficult process, which often took all day. Clotheslines were outside near the house and we can imagine Lila's frozen fingers when hanging laundry to dry in winter. Heavy irons sat heating on the stove ready for ironing wrinkles out of the clothes.

An icebox or icehouse to preserve food for short durations was necessary, but the tedious home canning of garden vegetables and fruits in glass jars, and drying or smoking meats and fish was also a part of farm life. These tasks were taken for granted in those days, but took a lot of time when measured by modern standards with our easy access to frozen and convenience foods.

From a well came water that could be dipped by bucket or, if it came through a pump, that pump needed to be primed. Often there was a pump inside the house and one outside. It was difficult to keep pipes from freezing in winter. Indoor plumbing was only a dream. The family shared an outhouse, an outside toilet that was certainly very cold in the winter and hot, smelly and buzzing with flies in the summer. Children had few toys. Some fortunate ones had wooden toys, such as rocking horses, wagons, sleds and small doll furniture. The girls treasured handmade dolls and doll clothes. Clothes for the family were made from cotton, wool, or other natural fibers. There were not many outfits, and often they were hand-me-downs. We can be sure they were practical and worn for work, church and school.[40]

---

[39] *Frontier House,* **PBS**
[40] *Frontier House,* **PBS**

CHARACTER

Education was usually limited to grammar school for farm children, and for some even grammar school was limited when farm work came first. Lila received a very good education in the one room schoolhouse near her farm on Archertown Road, and later at Professor Horner's Academy. Transportation was by foot, on horseback, in a horse-drawn carriage, or by boat or train. The era of the Model T Ford did not arrive until 1909 for Lila and Joseph, who were among the first families in New Egypt to own a car. Lila quickly learned to drive. Cars and driving opened new opportunities in her life.

As a child, Tom-boyish Lila exhibited versatility as she could hold her own playing baseball with her siblings and father after the chores were done. She was spiritually grounded in the earth and cared for the environment and animals in farming and later gardening. Lila was always concerned about the family cooperating and surviving together. Heartiness, endurance, cooperation, integrity, skills, and accepting people who were different, were among Robbins' family values. It was a greatly respected family by the wider community. Faith from within the Quaker tradition meant to them that with God's help, all was possible.[41] We will now examine how Lila became a part of the Thompson family and Joseph introduced her to politics.

CENTRALITY OF COMMUNICATIONS

Lila was always involved in communicating and working for more effective communications; she was a skilled elocutionist. All indications are that communication was a key ingredient in her attraction to Joseph M. Thompson. The tall handsome six-foot Joseph started as a young teenager as station agent for the Pennsylvania Railroad at Harvey Cedars, Ocean County, NJ, a position he held for five years. For another five years, Joseph was the chief telegrapher

---

[41] In Scripture, Acts 2 shows the effectiveness of the faith community surviving under oppression.

and station manager for the Union Transportation Company (UT) in New Egypt, later a vital part of the Jersey Central Railroad. Their courtship took place in 1890-91, before radio and telephone and in the middle of his employment with the railroads.

To place in perspective the importance of the telegraph and Morse Code in communication, Grandpa Joseph told me how during the Civil War, President Abraham Lincoln regularly sought relief from the White House pressure by going to the War Department's Telegraph Office, where Thomas T. Eckert, the chief telegrapher, received the latest war reports, and where, during one and one half years in 1861-62, Lincoln wrote the Emancipation Proclamation.[42] Grandpa emphasized how this document freed the slaves in the Confederate states in 1863, a world - changing event. Everywhere the telegraph office was the center of communication until well into the twentieth century. [43]

In New Egypt before 1900, it was in the UT telegraph office where news came from the rest of the world. Lila went there to learn the world news, to send messages and to travel on the train; it linked her to the world and to Joseph. At nineteen, two years before he could vote, Joseph managed the successful political campaign of an elected Plumsted Township Committeeman. A reform Republican at the time of the Populist Movement, Joseph helped move the Township from Democrat to reform Republican leadership and introduced Lila to the world of electoral politics. She had already seen fierce political in-fighting in churches, lodges, and civic organizations. Joseph also became Plumsted Township Clerk.[44]

THE ACADEMY

Another factor in their courtship was both Lila and Joseph attended Professor Horner's Classical Academy or Seminary, a high

---

[42] Verified, New York City Main Free Public Library Exhibit, Dec. 2001
[43] My Autobiography, from Thompson and Robbins family sources, 1951
[44] *My Autobiography,* 1951, from Thompson and Robbins family sources

school equivalent program. Both the Thompson and Robbins families emphasized education in the schools and on the farm. Lila and Joseph excelled at the academy, organized by the prominent and beloved Professor George D. Horner, a well-known Master in the Masonic Lodge and a pillar in the local Methodist Episcopal Church. He purchased the seminary (built in 1859) from the trustees of the Plumsted Institute in 1862 on 9-13 Front Street, New Egypt, a large boarding school building for boys and girls. Professor Horner lived in Wallin Tavern on part of the property. He was the sole manager of the "private school/academy" until his death in 1900. Lila enjoyed riding to school in the buckboard with her father, on the way to his blacksmith shop across the street from the academy. The academy honed the students' practical skills with academic skills so that students became excellent communicators. The academy emphasized the classics, practical lessons from the Bible, the three R's, and elocution training, which Lila and Joseph particularly enjoyed. They also learned not to be overly influenced by any one person or group. Professor Horner was an excellent mentor. As important as her farming background was to Lila, her academy education encouraged her to pursue other options for her life. [45]

Lila and Joseph's relationship blossomed in Professor Horner's Classical Academy. They shared their dreams with each other. Joseph wanted to be in politics and felt he could be the chief telegrapher in the US House of Representatives, as well as rise to the leadership of several lodges. They both wanted a family. Even in 1890, thirty years before women's suffrage, Lila envisioned her place was in the House or the Senate—New Jersey Legislature or even the USA Congress. Why? Because she cared about people, especially the downtrodden, the aged and the poor, and people responded to her leadership. Lila was a servant of the people. She felt her own positive influence growing up on the farm and in many organizations. Joseph

---

[45] K. Potter Interview, Claude Thompson Interviews, and UCLA Graduate School of Education, 1976; Dorothy S. Mount, p. 19; Church Bulletin, "One Hundredth Anniversary of the Methodist Church, New Egypt, NJ," 1951; and my acquaintance with South Jersey lodges and churches

saw Lila's effectiveness and always supported her efforts, often before his own. [46]

UNTIL DEATH DO US PART

Lila and Joseph married while they were teenagers. Rev. John Handley in Asbury Park Methodist Church, April 25, 1891, officiated at the wedding of the young couple, when Lila was sixteen and Joseph was nineteen. They honeymooned at the shore a few days before returning to New Egypt.

Romance, communication, and education remained central to their marriage and in her life's work. Forty-two years of life together in family, community and the world included their becoming the first husband and wife team in NJ politics. Who was Joseph?[47]

THE THOMPSON DIMENSION

Joseph was born December 17, 1871 in New Egypt and lived until January 7, 1948. He was the younger son of Rudolph W. (Rube) Thompson (born April 12, 1852, died 1932, at eighty years) and Elizabeth Murdock, (born November 1853 and died 1930 at seventy-six years). His older brother was William "Will" Thompson, who took care of cattle and farmed while Joseph studied the Bible, Morse code, public speaking, etc. at the Academy.

Several men from the Thompson family served with distinction in the Revolutionary Army, including an earlier ancestor, Colonel William Thompson. In family history the clan migrated from Scotland and Northern Ireland led by Anthony and John Thompson, first arriving in Boston, MA, June 26, 1637. Later descendents, led by James Thompson in about 1700, settled in Pleasure Bay near Asbury

---

[46] K. Potter and Claude Thompson *Interviews*; Rev. F. Elwood Perkins *Letter*, Oct. 18, 1977.
[47] *My Autobiography*, 1951

Park, NJ. The family has a coat of arms with the motto: "I wish for a fair fight." This old Scottish clan is derived from MacTavish, and spelled T-h-o-m-p-s-o-n in the Argyllshire area. [48]

From the time the railroad came along in the new nation the Thompsons became noted railroad pioneers. In 1828, Baltimore and Ohio Railroad began as the first operational railroad. In 1828, Bordentown, NJ's Camden and Amboy Railroad began construction and on Nov. 12, 1831, it became the second operational railroad.[49] Joseph's legacy was to continue that pioneering spirit and much more. It is noteworthy that Joseph's father, Rube, the town crier, walked through New Egypt announcing through a megaphone the film to be shown at John Meirs' Hall/Theater, 10 Front Street, and the starting time, "Come one, come all, Big and small, To see the movie, In Meirs' Hall."[50]

Kenny Potter reported when he was a child in one of the few times he stayed with Joseph and Lila, she proposed going out to buy a meal for Kenny. Joseph's reply stayed with Kenny, "Do you think we are made of money?" They ate leftovers at the Thompson homestead that night. It did not seem fair to Kenny, with all the Potters had given Claude Thompson at their farm the many times he stayed there.[51] In my experience, my grandfather was always generous with me.

HUSBAND JOSEPH, THE POLITICIAN

Joseph had a vision of service in politics. After being Chief Telegrapher for the Union Transportation Railroad Company in New Egypt, my grandfather spent more than twenty-five years in

---

[48] Thompson Family Origin (description) and Coat of Arms (Crest: An arm embowered in armor, holding the truncheon of a broken lance; Arms: A fess counter embattled between three falcons); Railroad Museum of PA, Railroad History Time Line, by Kurt R. Bell, Archivist; Carol Comegno, Courier-Post Staff, South Jersey Courier Post © 2000.
[49] Ibid
[50] Mount, Dorothy S. p.20
[51] Kenny Potter *Interview*, 2000

Washington, D.C., where, appointed by Congressman Howell, Joseph became Chief Telegrapher of the House of Representatives, and Chief Republican Page in the US House, during the administrations of Presidents William McKinley, Theodore Roosevelt, William Howard Taft, and Woodrow Wilson. At that time, Thomas Jefferson's lengthy guide to parliamentary procedure was in vogue. Joseph studied it thoroughly and then wrote the much more useable *Short Form Parliamentary Guide*[52] for use by legislative bodies, fraternal orders and clubs. From observing the many speakers in the US House of Representatives, he enhanced his speaking skills, with everyone clear on his emphasis. He used his sense of humor, such as when he kicked up his foot to make sure the audience got the point.[53]

Joseph served as State Councilor of the Jr. Order of United American Mechanics (Jr. OUAM), a patriotic lodge, State and National Councilor of Daughters of America and was prominent in that period of history of the New Egypt Methodist Episcopal Church.

He successfully managed the New Egypt Cornhuskers baseball team for several seasons. During one game, word reached him that a son, Claude, was born at home. He took the nearest bicycle and sped across town for home. The bicycle's owner thought his bike had been stolen, but later was forgiving when he found that Joseph had borrowed it for that emergency.[54]

MARRIAGE AND FAMILY

After their wedding, April 25, 1891, in their early marriage, Lila was still a teenager, five feet five inches tall, active, slender and beautiful. She liked to have fun. Six foot tall Joseph always wore a derby hat. Sometimes he would come into the house and forget to take

---

[52] *Short Form Parliamentary Guide,* published and distributed by the Ocean County Board of Chosen Freeholders, Toms River, NJ, 1926
[53] Elizabeth Miers Morgan *Interview*, 1998
[54] *My Autobiography*, My Ancestors, (Joseph and Lila Robbins Thompson) 1951

his hat off. She'd take one look at him, kick up past his nose and catch the rim of his hat, sending it right off his head.[55]

It was two and one half years after their wedding before they had a child. Then Lila focused her time on their children: Sewell Murdock, born October 25, 1893, Joseph Carlton, April 8, 1900, and my dad, Milton Claude, August 12, 1905. She also gave major help to Rube & Elizabeth Thompson in raising their adopted son, William Gibberson, about the same age as Sewell. Lila and her siblings also helped raise brother Theodore, Jr, "Dory" Robbins' children, when both "Dory" and his wife died from complications of the disease of alcoholism. Lila also took in a domestic worker, a girl, to whom she paid a salary for house chores.[56]

In 1907-08, Joseph, continuing as a Page in the US House of Representatives, moved the family to Washington, D.C. Living in the nation's capitol was a hardship on the family. In less than two years they moved their residence back to New Egypt, while Joseph continued to work in Washington, shuttling back and forth on the train. The Thompson homestead was built shortly before 1900 at 39 North Main Street and Lakewood Road, across from the Methodist Church. It was a large two-story, neat, very comfortable home completely surrounded by an airy porch. Carlton and Claude were born at home, as was the custom then. Lila had a workroom, a sitting room, a dining room, a parlor, and other functional rooms, all arranged so comfortably that Claude loved the homestead more than any other dwelling in which he lived.[57]

It was a major jolt to Lila, when three-year-old Claude was stricken by pneumonia. Illness dominated much of his pre-school life, and being the youngest, he was babied a lot. No oxygen or miracle

[55] Fote, Linda. *Interview* with M. Claude Thompson, NE, Feb. 1983, for National Organization of Women (NOW), *Ocean County Women: Makers of History*
[56] Claude Thompson taped *Interview*, 1976
[57] 1976 & 1986 *Interviews*: I slept in part of the homestead, Claude's apartment where he wished to die; he died in the Masonic Home in Burlington instead.

drugs were available in 1908-09. Bedridden for three months, Claude hovered between life and death, under the care of a Methodist Cuban Dr. Morin. Once when Lila's brother Charles Robbins, a strong worker and boxer, visited, he wept bitterly, for Claude's back was twisted in a curve like a "Philadelphia pretzel." God, prayer, Lila, and the doctor's care pulled Claude through the worst of the crisis. Then Dr. Morin commanded, "You'll have to get a back brace for Claude!" Lila refused, saying, "If I get him a brace, he will never get rid of it for the rest of his life." She daily applied hot mustard packs that almost took the skin off Claude's back and massaged him with Witch Hazel, while praying unceasingly. After more than a year of Lila's dedicated care, Claude's back straightened and strengthened. Claude called her a "miracle worker," for he was later able to play football, basketball, baseball, wrestle, run track, especially the one hundred yard dash, lift heavy bodies as a funeral director and for hours hold his son (me) on his shoulders at parades. Lila and Claude bonded in a most special relationship for all his lifetime. From a teenager on, Claude loved to dance and Lila always wanted him to teach her to waltz. Dad always regretted that he never taught her to dance. [58]

No sooner was Claude better, than Carlton, never a strong child, became severely ill at age nine with childhood diseases of the turn of the century. With no vaccinations to prevent infections, or miracle drugs to cure them, Carlton hovered between life and death and died on August 7, 1909, five days before Claude's fourth birthday. The family was overwhelmed with grief. Carlton was the image of Lila and had all her calm and goodness. Lila bore the brunt of his death, lost weight and was diagnosed by Dr. Morin to have spots on her lungs. Her strength seemed to be sapped away by the tragic loss. Lila missed lodge and Republican meetings due to her distress. It was as if she wanted to die; Lila was thirty-four years old. [59]

---

[58] From 1936-1941, Claude held me on his shoulders at Philadelphia Thanksgiving Parades and always told me the story of recovery from curvature of the back.

[59] Claude Thompson *Interviews, 1976, 1978 1983, 1985, 1986*

TRAVEL, RECOVERY, AND SERVICE

Joseph returned permanently from Washington and they bought one of the first cars in New Egypt, a Model T Ford Touring Car. Son Sewell drove to Mt. Holly and bought a driver's license; there was no test in those days. Sewell did the driving as they traveled the dirt and gravel roads. The only protection on the sides of the Model T was curtains. Lila enjoyed the outings. Claude was eager to go and all three enjoyed Joseph's stories when he went along. The New Egypt Press was filled with reports of the Thompsons' special travels by car to the shore and other areas of New Jersey and USA in that period after Carlton's death. By God's grace, fresh air, nourishing fresh foods, time taken and change of scenery meant that Lila worked through her grief and recovered completely. The spots on her lungs disappeared, her weight returned to normal, her caring for others returned and, most importantly, Lila's great gift of transmitting life forces, along with her calm supportive goodness, returned and grew. Through her faith in God, Lila affirmed, "I don't stop loving when I grieve their death or miss them desperately!" [60]

At that time, Joseph was National Councilor, following his term as State Councilor of the Daughters of America (D of A). Men could still hold D of A offices then. He insisted that Lila attend the National Convention in Atlanta with him. Joseph instituted the Orphans' Fund of the D of A. Then as now, there was a great need to care for children without parents. Joseph was selected to direct the new agency, a position he could have easily managed, but as he often did, knowing his wife's capabilities, he facilitated the advent of Lila, asking, "Why don't you make Lila the Director?" Thus she became the Director of the D of A's Orphan's Fund. She earned $60. each month and directed the fund until her death. Joseph was aware that

---

[60] "Way Back When" columns weekly in the *New Egypt Press*, 1974 - 1978 originally printed 1909—1913, were filled with Lila, Joseph, Sewell and Claude's trips; Claude Thompson *Interviews*.

she probably did a better job than he would have done. She became National Councilor, D of A, at their Philadelphia Convention, 1913. [61]

Crises lay ahead. World War I (WWI) to "Make the World Safe for Democracy" descended upon Europe in 1914. The USA entered WWI in 1917 through Nov. 11, 1918, Armistice Day. Lila's oldest son, Sewell, enlisted in the US Army and was deployed in active service abroad. Lila held a special spot in her heart for her first born, Sewell. Throughout the war the dangers in the trenches of Europe were rivaled by threats at home from German submarines. New Jersey was on alert facing the Atlantic Ocean, as well as monitoring air traffic, with Lakehurst Air Base in Ocean County, a major International Air Terminal in this time of increasing airplane and dirigible travel.[62] As a patriotic mother of a soldier, Lila prayed and worried, "Am I to lose another son, my special strong and talented Sewell, to war?"

An athlete, Sewell had been self-sufficient. We would say 'self-actualized' today. He married Ethel Chafey, November 7, 1912. Before WWI, Dec. 1914, NJ Assemblyman Conrad gave Sewell a legislative assistant job in Trenton. In 1915, he was the star third baseman on the Morrisville, PA and Toms River, NJ baseball teams in the semi-pro Delaware River League. Sewell then pursued a professional baseball career in the Philadelphia Athletics' farm system in the old Eastern League in Elmira, New York, at the specific hand written invitation from Connie Mack, the owner-manager of the A's dated Jan. 4, 1916: "Would advise that you accept the offer at once from the Class B Club…Best wishes, Yours Very Truly, Connie Mack."[63] Sewell made an all out effort in Elmira, the A's minor league affiliate, when WWI interrupted his professional baseball career, but gratefully his life was spared. After WWI, he came back to Lila, Joseph and Claude's open arms. Having divorced his first wife, Sewell found the love of his life, Marion McGinley, and they were

---

[61] Ibid.
[62] *An Encyclopedia of World History, p.*938 and following, outlines WWI
[63] American Base Ball Club, Connie Mack's *Letter* to Sewell Thompson, Jan.4, 1916; NE Press clippings through 1915, and Dec. 18, 1914

married August 31, 1919. The extended family lived in the Thompson homestead in New Egypt. Sewell followed a successful career in business, later moving to Vincentown, NJ. He divorced again, married a third time, and had no children. [64]

Even when the children were young there were problems in Lila and Joseph's marriage, but in those days couples stayed together. It was not surprising that handsome Joseph gave into temptation, drinking and other women, with all his time away working in Washington, DC. In addition, his lodge and political activities took him to many other cities. Meanwhile, Lila worked closer to home or traveled to different cities. Son Claude confirmed this in writing: "Dad was quite a sport and chased around a lot. Mother knew this and told me she had thoughts of leaving him but we children were young and she did not want to split the family. In later years when we were older, she said it was too late and she still loved him, in spite of all this."[65]

In fairness to Joseph, it was extremely difficult to be married to such a good person as Lila. She was always forgiving and accepting of him, and perhaps he did not feel worthy, sometimes even resenting her. His untreated disease of alcoholism infected the whole family and his other relationships. He was a functional alcoholic, taking his work and other responsibilities seriously. I can still remember Grandpa Joseph picking up a flask of vinegar, thinking it was iced tea, drinking from it, and vomiting on Mom's carefully prepared holiday meal, because he had been drinking before he arrived at our house. In spite of the disease, he was not abusive; he was always attentive and loving toward me. Joseph died when I was almost twelve years old, giving us those years together.

In addition Lila had a weight problem from the time of the beginning of World War I until her death. That era's photographs

---

[64] *USA Census*, 1920, listed Lila, Joseph, Claude, Sewell and wife Marian as residents at 39 North Main Street, New Egypt and *Family Bible*
[65] Claude Thompson *Letter*, Nov. 2, 1977

indicate Lila was heavy. Almost all the lodge meetings were followed by dinners. I vividly remember my parents bringing home substantial amounts of food, rich in white flour and sugar, and sandwiches and desserts that increased Dad's waistline and salved my teenage hunger. It is called compulsive overeating and especially we non-drinking Thompsons, including Lila, ate more than our share. Overeaters Anonymous teaches that addictiveness to food is just as cunning and baffling a disease as addiction to alcohol. Lila and the rest of the family were far from perfect.

NOTHING STOPPED LILA

A story my father, Claude, often repeated about Lila was her clothesline story. Lila attended many meetings and one dark winter night, she was racing out the back door of their New Egypt home, through the back yard toward Main Street for a meeting at the New Egypt Methodist Church. In the darkness of no moon and no electric lights, she did not see the clothesline. The line caught Lila under her chin and her momentum literally lifted her off the ground. Abruptly, she fell. There she was, flat on her back - stunned and sore. Knowing that her presence at the meeting was important, she picked herself up, brushed herself off and went on to lead a successful church board meeting. Lila was not a complainer and never even mentioned the incident at the meeting. She was a woman of true grit.[66]

RISING ABOVE CUSTOM

In an era when many astute and persevering women were fighting for rights that white men already enjoyed, Lila emerged as a stateswoman far ahead of her time. In one historical article about Lila, the heading is: Joseph M. Thompson, subsuming Lila under her husband's name. However, from such reports in printed articles where editorial custom routinely listed her as Mrs. Joseph M. Thompson, she did not allow herself to be controlled by her husband or party

---

[66] Claude Thompson *Interview,* 1976

officials, even those who had given her major support in her elections. Lila's roots and character made all the difference. She was her own person and her legacy stands on its own. She was a "Woman for All Seasons!"[67]

LILA AND WOMEN'S SUFFRAGE

The Movement for Women's Suffrage began before the Civil War, in conjunction with the Abolitionist Movement against slavery. Actually, New Jersey's Constitution ratified by the Provisional Congress in Burlington, July 2, 1776, gave "all inhabitants...worth fifty pounds proclamation money" the right to vote. The first women allowed to vote were widows and unmarried women who had inherited property from soldiers killed in the Revolution. Wives could not vote as they did not meet the property requirement, since everything belonged to their husbands. Voting women were falsely blamed for the fraud-filled election of 1807. The adoption of the provision, "no person except free white males could vote," followed. Women's voting was rescinded. About 10,000 NJ women had voted 1776-1807. [68]

New York and NJ women and men were prominent in the movement for Women's Suffrage, especially in the historic Seneca Falls Women's organizing Meeting of 1898. [69]

A special election to amend the NJ Constitution was conducted in 1915 to permit women to vote. New Egypt had support with John F. Fort, the prominent son of the former NJ Governor George F. Fort, promoting the amendment. It did not pass in New

---

[67] Alfred Heston, *HISTORY OF SOUTH JERSEY*, p. 53-54

[68] *Asbury Park Press*, Nov. 4, 1996, Rossbach, Nancy, "N.J. women were first in country to vote, A Look Back—An Historical Vignette"

[69] Held in NY with NJ well represented: Miller, Pauline S., *Ocean County Four Centuries in the Making*, p.694-97

Egypt, but did pass in Ocean County, the only county of the 21 in the state to do so. *The New York Times* lauded Ocean County's support.[70]

The Nineteenth Amendment to the Constitution, granting women the right to vote, passed with the thirty-six required states, NJ among them, on August 26, 1920. NJ's first two women, Margaret B. Laird, Newark, and Jennie C. Van Ness, East Orange, Republicans, were elected to the General Assembly from Essex County two and one half months later, opening the way for more women to be elected.[71]

In New Egypt, Lila supported a woman's right to vote from before the 1915 contest onward. She became involved in Republican politics when she was selected Vice Chair of the Ocean County Republican Party Committee and the Ocean County Republican Women's Committee. She also was selected a member of the State Republican Party Committee and the State Republican Women's Committee, two of the most influential NJ political groups.[72] This dedicated humanitarian was at the right time and the right place. She had a vision of cooperative caring for and with people in the electoral political arena.

LEADERSHIP

Her involvements in caring for others were many and most significant for the time. Lila became an officer in fraternal lodges on the local, state and national levels including, but not limited to, the Order of the Eastern Star, the Order of Pocahontas (The Red Ladies), the American Legion Auxiliary, D of A, etc. She was an active member and officer in her church, New Egypt Methodist Episcopal and the first woman Chair of the governing board, the Board of Stewards. Lila's Republican Party involvement is noted above. She

---

[70] Miller, Pauline S., p.694-5; *New York Times*, Oct. 23, 1915
[71] *New Jersey Women In The Legislature, Unique Voices, Unique Service*, A Commemorative Digest, Sept. 12, 1995, p.13,16,19
[72] Miller, Pauline S., p. 697 and *New Jersey Women In The Legislature*, p.22

was active in forming public institutions, organizing the Ocean County Public Library and becoming the first woman Foreman in the USA of a grand jury. In the family she received what we call 'foster children' today and always helped needy members. Lila was known for her special caring for the bodies of New Egyptians when they died.[73]

In and around New Egypt, Lila did the preliminary preparations and caring for bodies of the deceased. She took this seriously and Claude often told the story of the death of Mrs. Cowperthwait. Lila was attired in her formal gown and was just leaving for a special banquet in Newark where she was to be the honored guest. The telephone rang. Lila answered and heard, "Mrs. Cowperthwait just died. We need you to prepare the body before the undertaker arrives." Without hesitation, Lila donned a full apron over her gown and hurried to the home where she prepared the body. This important tradition included washing and diapering the body as well as comforting the family who just lost a loved one. Thus she arrived late at the banquet and assured them that her duties to the deceased and her family came first. These acts of kindness and concern help us understand what a compassionate woman Lila was. [74]

Equally important was her vision for wider public service bringing all she was to the reality of the political arena as a "reform Republican." Willa Cather wrote in *O Pioneers!* (1913) and *My Antonia* (1918) a land myth (geography uninhabited by humans) and a land goddess to rule it (bringing order out of chaos): a noble, creative, strong, patient, robust, sensitive and enduring woman who undergoes a symbolic courtship with the land, but at last she is able to dominate it.[75] Lila as a farmer's daughter was nurtured by the land beside the Pine Barrens, and later led the way in highway construction and humanizing legislation.

---

[73] Claude Thompson, Taped *Interview* by me, 1976

[74] Claude was very passionate about his mother's caring, Taped *Interview*, 1976

[75] Hoffman, Frederick J., *The 20's, American Writing in the Postwar Decade*, p.182

COUNTY LIBRARY

Map: Ocean County, NJ, by Ocean County Library; Townships added.

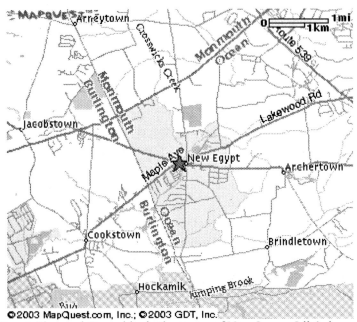

New Egypt, Plumsted Township, in the center of New Jersey, Lila's home town;
Map provided by MapQuest.com, Inc.

Father Theodore Robbins, Sr., ca. middle 1800's, by Egan and Colloway, Phila.

Mother Lydia A. Hankins Robbins, ca. middle 1800's, by Egan and Colloway, Phila.

Bottom Photo: Pine View Farm and Boarding House, brother William Robbins
owner. People came from miles around to stay there. Destroyed by fire Feb. 1976.
Top Photo: Theodore Robbins, Sr. Farm as it looks in 2002, ravaged by time

Pensive Lila, by Thomas M. Asson, New Egypt.

Handsome young Joseph M. Thompson, by Thomas M. Asson, New Egypt, NJ.

Son Carlton Thompson, 1909, by Thomas M. Asson.

Sewell Thompson in World War I Army uniform, 1918.

Left to right. 1. Jennie Trimmer (Sewell's wife), Lila, and Irene (the only one Lila knew as Claude's wife) Thompson. 2. Sewell, Lila and Claude Thompson. 1932

Lila and Joseph; foster child Wilbur Childers and sister Winnie.

Lila and Joseph Thompson Home, shortly before 1900-1935, facing Lakewood Road at North Main Street, New Egypt. Claude Thompson returned to live in first floor apartment, 1978-86, by Thomas M. Asson, New Egypt.

New Egypt Methodist Episcopal Church building and Official Board, about 1940;
Claude Thompson on far left, top row by Church sign.

Triluminar Chapter No. 243, OES, Newark, NJ, Officers, 1930-31; L. to R., Back row standing, L. to R. Tessie Newmark, Lila McCarron, Augusta Franklin, Mae Price, Florence Futterman, George Gee; Middle Row standing, Alice Hayat, Matilda Ward, Maude Freeman, Benjamin Ward, Eugenie Lomax, Jeanette Kessel, Lottie Davis, Lillian Dresdner; Front Row, sitting, Florence Simpson, Elizabeth Valentine, Mabel Biggs, Lila W. Thompson (Past Grand Matron), Wilhelmina Best, Esther Solomon, by Valentine, Newark.

Donald C. Thompson

Lila and other conventioneers stroll the Boardwalk at Order of the Eastern Star (OES) Convention, Atlantic City, NJ, 1932.

Historic photo of the NJ Legislature: General Assembly, 1924 or 1925; Lila is standing left center in the Assembly's chamber.

Left to Right, President Calvin Coolidge, unidentified woman, Lila, and NJ Governor Edge, 1925.

April, 1929.

Presented to

O. E. S. Home of N.J.

By

Lila W. Thompson

P. G. M.

Lila inscribed Bible. She presented numerous Bibles to the OES Home residents in Bernardsville.

1930's Buick. Lila died driving home from work, April 3, 1933.

Lila loved horses. Shown with the horse and buggy, common mode of transportation in south Jersey into the 1920's.

Lila Funeral, April 8, 1933; casket surrounded by a small portion of the flowers sent to pay tribute to her; largest funeral in Ocean County to that time, by Thomas M. Asson, New Egypt.

Lila in evening gown, with necklace and corsage, her best known picture, in 1930, by Thomas M. Asson, New Egypt.

Don at the Lila Highway Monument and Marker, US Route 9 at Adelphia Road, reads: LILA W. THOMPSON HIGHWAY: So named by Act of the New Jersey Legislature, Jan. 15, 1934; In memory of Lila W. Thompson, Ocean County's Assemblywoman; Through her efforts while a member of the Legislature the state road from Adelphia to Lakewood was constructed. Dedicated May 26, 1934.

Lila's surviving nephew and former Mayor of New Egypt, Kenneth Potter and niece, Mildred Potter Ivins in 1998, in Mildred's home, New Egypt.

Left to right, Irene, Donald and Claude Thompson, about 1940, by Thomas M. Asson, New Egypt.

CHAPTER FIVE

THE GREAT ELECTION OF 1923

"Jesus said, 'Follow me and you will know the truth and the truth will make you free.'" (John 8:31-32, RSV)[76]

Citing the background forces of the changing world after World War I, Chapter Five reflects on the roots of Lila's success, as well as the invigorating Primary Election and General Election campaigns of 1923, resulting in Lila's election to the General Assembly.

BACKGROUND: ROOTS OF SUCCESS

TRAILBLAZING

Lila became involved in numerous lodges, the Republican Party, the Methodist Episcopal Church and other community groups, and was elected to local, state and national offices. With all these organizations in decline in 2002, except the Republican Party, it is difficult to recapture their importance from 1891-1933, an era when radio first became national in 1925 and television was a subject of science fiction.

Consider lodges, or secret fraternal orders. I was a member of the Junior Order of United American Mechanics (Jr.OUAM) joining at age sixteen. Jr.OUAM was one of the leading patriotic men's organizations in Lila's time; Joseph and Claude were State Councilors and Lila was an officer in the Auxiliary. Although my father expected me to follow in their footsteps, I chose another direction: the church. Lodges practice a secret ritual in their meetings, with a black ball

---

[76] *The New Testament in Four Versions: Revised Standard,* Christianity Today, p.296

system for choosing members, advocate conservative patriotic and religious values, charge dues, expect formal attire at meetings, require a good amount of time for participation, and do service in their communities. For previous generations, lodges and other community organizations were essential parts of life. Hundreds of members would gather from all over the state for special occasions, such as state officer visitations. It was a way to climb the social and organizational ladder; it was networking and developing leadership and speaking skills. Sewell was active in the non-secret American Legion as an Army veteran of WWI: Lila was active in the Auxiliary, having risen to first Vice President at the time of her election to the NJ Assembly in 1923. [77]

However, her first major lodge involvement was in the influential Daughters of America, (D of A). She was a member of Oakford Council No. 16 in New Egypt. Lila served two terms as State Councilor of NJ. The state D of A, under Lila's Councillorship, made a net gain from 2938 to 3386 members in one term, the largest net gain reported by any state Councilor. Lila and Joseph were National Councilors of D of A. Lila became Associate National Councilor in 1903 and National Councilor in 1913, holding her National Session in Philadelphia in 1913. She was National Manager of the Orphans Department, the state orphanages of the D of A, for over twenty years until her death. Lila spoke and traveled in more than forty states for the benefit of orphans and the promotion of D of A. She was one of their most attractive speakers and leaders in a time when the organization grew rapidly.[78]

The Degree of Pocahontas (Red Ladies), a prominent organization in that time selected Lila in 1913 as State Chair/Chief Minnehaha, a very busy lodge year for her. Then the members unanimously declared, "Lila's the one for Secretary, the Great Keeper of Records." She held this position for nineteen years, until her death.

---

[77] Claude Thompson *Letter*, Oct. 18, 1977; *NE Press, Oct. 23, 1914*
[78] Claude Thompson *Letter*, Nov. 2, 1977; Pauline S. Miller, p.697-98; *NE Press, Sept. 8, 1911*

She danced the Native American installation services. Lila served in a state office with the Improved Order of Red Men.[79]

In 2003 these Native American labels are offensive and take on racist overtones. For example, Stanford University realized the problem and changed its teams' names from Indians to Cardinals. This awareness is now obvious.

Lila joined the exceedingly important Order of the Eastern Star (OES), companion group of the Masonic Order, in 1914 in Lakewood. She organized the Sphinx Chapter No. 130, New Egypt OES on July 6, 1920, became its first Grand Matron and served two terms. The state Grand Matron, Sarah E. Marshall, appointed Lila as NJ Grand Esther. Then OES selected Lila the Grand Matron of the state in 1927. Mr. Cruise Hughes was her Grand Master. Claude, who sang and used sleight of hand (magic) in all four of their receptions, testified they were marvelous together and are still remembered fondly in OES circles. Lila did not stop there. She organized several other OES Chapters in NJ, including the Lila W. Thompson Chapter, OES #242, 825 Broad Street, Newark. She established the OES Retirement Home in Bernardsville and served on its Board of Directors for five years, concluding with being chairperson at the time of her death, 1933.[80]

Her organizational repertoire also included state positions in the Degree of Rebecca, the Sons and Daughters of Liberty, and the Auxiliary of the Jr. OUAM, for whom Joseph had been State Councilor in 1909. She organized the Women's Branch of the NJ Historical Society and played a key role in the organization of the Ocean County Historical Society, serving as its chairperson.[81]

---

[79] Claude Thompson *Interview, 1976*

[80] Lila was among the founding members and the driving force in the 1920 creation of NE Sphinx Chapter, as well as several other chapters, *NE Press*, (cont.) June 28, 1923; Claude Thompson *Interview*, 1983 and *Letter*, Nov. 2, 1977; Photographs of Lila with the Newark Chapter, OES.

[81] Claude Thompson *Letter*, Nov. 2, 1977; *Trenton Evening Times*, Oct.11,1950, Miller, Pauline S. p.698

Paul Kimball Hospital Board of Managers, Lakewood, depended on the organizing by key member, Lila, for its survival in the Great Depression. It seems a quaint name now, but membership on the Board of Managers of the Mothers' Congress was especially significant in an age of great need, when women and children were abused in slave labor working conditions. She organized and was the first chairperson of the Ocean County Free Library, 1924.[82]

As noted earlier, Theodore Robbins, Sr. was a Quaker, but there was no Friends Meeting in New Egypt and most of the Robbins siblings went to the Plumsted (New Egypt) Presbyterian Church. When Lila and Joseph married in 1891, she joined his church, the New Egypt Methodist Episcopal Church. She sang in the choir and taught Sunday School classes in her teenage and young adult years. A regular worship participant at the Sunday Evening Services, she sat on the right side toward the front and was one of the first to tithe her income, which was not taken lightly, but was a sacrifice in those hard economic times.[83] She was the first woman president of the New Egypt Methodist Episcopal Church Board of Stewards, truly groundbreaking in that time of almost complete male dominance of the church. More than that, "Lila Thompson was a servant of the people...rather than a politician," noted her last pastor, Rev. Perkins. She was a "reform Republican."[64] Methodists were the largest denomination in Congress and state Legislatures throughout her lifetime.

Lila's other influential organizations included the Ocean County Republican Committee (vice-chair, 1920), and Ocean County Republican Women's Club (1922); NJ Republican Committee (representing Ocean County, 1920; committeewoman 1921-22) and NJ Republican Women's Club, Board of Governors (1922-23). She served on the Ocean County Grange, the Parent Teachers'

---

[82] Ibid
[83] Claude Thompson *Letter*, Nov. 2, 1977
[64] Rev. F. Elwood Perkins *Letter*, Oct. 18, 1977

Association, and the Toms River Trust Company. She was indeed a community leader.[85]

In addition, Lila was the first woman foreman (forewoman) of a Grand Jury in the USA, a monumental achievement. Ocean County Judge Harry Newman appointed her the first forewoman, preceding a woman appointed in Texas by one to two months. As a forewoman of the Grand Jury, Lila learned even more how to make just decisions under pressure, especially for poor people and those in great need.[86]

When she spoke in Baltimore, one listener insisted, "We want you to speak to our 'City Fathers.' " They were called an old English term, "The Selectmen" for city councilmen. Thus Lila was the first woman to speak to "The Selectmen" in Baltimore, MD. She spoke on a beautiful platform in the shape of a pavilion, with no other women present and where none had ever spoken before.[87]

Lila was a first in many things and yet it never went to her head. She remained affectionate with her sons, other family members and friends. By 1923, she was already extensively involved and thus well known in lodge, church, and political work: the first factor in her election as the first woman official in all of Ocean County. Joseph did not mind her groundbreaking achievements. In fact he enabled some of them, such as manager of the Orphan's Department, D of A. She, in teamwork with husband Joseph, the politician, could reach the needed support for election through organizing members and friends she knew throughout Ocean County and beyond.

Some have asked how she had time for her family. Her three sons were spaced over twelve years. By 1910, Sewell was seventeen years old and owned and operated poolrooms and bowling alleys until he sold them in 1914; he married in 1912. Carlton died in 1909, only nine years old. Claude, thirteen in 1918 at the end of WWI, was the

---

[85] Miller, Pauline S. p. 697,698
[86] *My Autobiography*, 1951: Ancestors
[87] Claude Thompson Tape *Interview*, 1976

son affected by his parents' absences. Lila chose foster child, Wilbur Childers, in 1924, as she began her second term in the Assembly.

The African and Native-American traditions of taking a village to raise a child were operational then in New Egypt, with neighbors, grandparents, aunts and uncles watching out for Claude and later, Wilbur. Dad told how money was left at home for him when his parents were away. New Egypt restaurants and grocery stores, as instructed by Lila and Joseph, kept credit for Claude's eating expenses when he was alone, and he learned how to cook for himself. He seldom got into difficulties, but he confessed to some youthful pranks, such as throwing rocks on the tin roof of the Main Street Bowling Alley when the pinsetters were trying to work, and on the Isis Movie Theater roof, when the managers were trying to sleep. Similar exploits on the Potter farm were directed toward the hired hand in the barn, who didn't even like to see Claude walk down the lane. Dad commented with a whimsical smile, "I was generally trustworthy." You could say he was one of the first "latch key" children, but according to Claude, "It helped me develop independence and responsibility." This was particularly true when he took care of Wilbur. When Carlton died, Lila learned how to drive. When the Legislature was in session she took Claude to stay with her two days a week in the Stacy Trent Hotel in Trenton.[90]

When together, the family enjoyed leisure at the shore, picnics and swimming at a nearby lake, and baseball. Joseph managed the New Egypt Cornhuskers team; Claude, nicknamed "Dick," following Sewell, played baseball and all enjoyed watching the national pastime at ballparks like Shibe Park, the home of the Philadelphia Phillies and Athletics. Claude, billed as "The Boy Wizard," shared magic shows, danced and sang to entertain.[89]

---

[90] Claude Thompson *Interview* with Linda Fote, for NOW, Feb. 1983 and recorded *Interview*, Nov. 1976; Kenneth Potter *Interview*, 2001; *NE Press,* Oct. 23, 1914

[89] Claude Thompson, recorded *Interview*, Nov., 1976, over 60 years as a magician, and sang until his last days in the Masonic Home Choir

WOMEN IN POLITICS

The second factor in Lila's election was the rising tide of women in previously denied Legislative halls. With the election of Margaret Laird and Jennie Van Ness, the two Essex County Republican women to the NJ General Assembly (Assembly), the previously all white male club was opened to women in 1921. Meanwhile, Lillian Felckert was named vice-chair of the NJ Republican Committee and founded the NJ Republican Women's Club and county clubs in 1922. She appointed Lila and another woman to the NJ Republican Committee (1920) and one woman to each of the twenty-one county committees, including Lila in Ocean (vice chair, 1920).

Lila was prominent in the Republican Party, for the Republicans immediately drew in the middle class native-born Protestant white women of the suffrage movement. Later, as the women achieved elective office, Mrs. Felckert made demands of them.[90] The positive women's thrust prepared the way for Lila's election to the Assembly and her inner strength kept her free from others' attempted matriarchal dominance.

STATESWOMAN

The stateswoman quality Lila exuded was the third factor in her election. In a "man's world" she knew how to lead. "She was not a politician like husband Joseph, she was a stateswoman and thus very electable," commented one living witness. Lila was a person of honesty and integrity, with a gentle, yet firm spirit nurtured in the soil. She treated people equally from all walks of life, from the most humble to the greatest: her motivation was for their well-being, not her own. This astute woman was a mediator who often worked out "small town wars" and disputes, so those involved felt satisfied with

---

[90] Lillian Felckert put Lila in party positions that helped her get elected and in the 1924 legislative session demanded Lila support a bill to remove NJ Education Commissioner from Governor's control. *NE Press*, Feb. 7, 1924

the process and the results of settlement. She was full of calm and goodness, mixed with a spark of charisma and spiritual depth.[91]

In contrast, many politicians tend to operate out of self-interest, greed, revenge, and control, always looking to re-election and willing to twist the truth to get there, sometimes stingy or covetous, often tending to be angry with opponents and sometimes friendly with gambling, bootlegging and corruption. Narcissistic, they have swelled heads about their own importance. Lila, whose temperament was different, was not at all that way, but Joseph did have a track record as a politician. Joseph lost to T. Frank Appleby for US Congressman from the third NJ district in an earlier election.[92]

Interviews with living witnesses verify what I have always known. Elizabeth Miers Morgan observed, "Lila was a rare person. She was mild, calm and thoughtful. She did her job with heart and soul." Ann Ryan reminisced, "I remember Lila very well. She was well known for her honesty. I believe she always spoke the truth."[93]

"THE TIMES, THEY ARE A-CHANGIN' "

The situation in the USA was changing. Some factors were used to oppose Lila's election. At the end of the nineteenth century, especially in 1898, the USA emerged as a militaristic imperialistic power, acquiring Alaska, taking Hawaii, Guam, Puerto Rico, and the Philippines (in a decade long bloody war) while holding sway in Cuba and Mexico. WWI followed smaller wars and produced new ones, as

---

[91] Kenneth Potter, nephew of Lila and Joseph, lifetime resident of New Egypt and 39 year Plumsted Township Committeeman, mostly as Mayor, *Interview* 1998

[92] In 1964-66 securing passage of Nevada and USA Civil Rights and Voting Rights laws, I clearly saw the differences between statespersons and politicians.

[93] Elizabeth Miers Morgan, *Interview* 1998 in Forked River, born and raised in New Egypt, and 89 years old in 2002. Ann Ryan, a 91-year-old lifetime resident of New Egypt, speaking at the NE Historical Society meeting, June 26, 2002.

it did not "make the world safe for democracy," but shook old political foundations. At home, a second industrial revolution resulted in huge industrial expansion that included NJ and brought mass immigration to the USA. It produced the rise of rich aristocracy in opposition to the growing trade unionist movement to defend workers' rights, including protecting women and children. The militarism and industrialism of greed shattered the older optimistic beliefs that the world was getting better and better. The "make the world safe for democracy" cry spurred women to lead the charge to assert their gifts in new areas of influence (Legislatures and Congress) to protect children from abuse in work, education or orphanages, to find care for the elderly, veterans and others destitute before and during the Great Depression, 1929-30's. [94] Lila was ready to lead the charge.

THE KLAN ONSLAUGHT

Another area of issue was the major influx of the Ku Klux Klan into New Jersey in 1923. They attended church services in South Jersey in such great numbers that they were able to speak their message of patriotism mixed with racist, anti-immigrant (especially those from Greece, Italy and the Balkans), anti-Catholic and anti-Semitic hatred and exclusion. The Klan was so appealing that Lila's son Claude later admitted, "At age eighteen, I almost joined the Klan because of their strong message of patriotism."[95] Editor Addison Moore astutely observed: "So far as church organizations (KKK included) are concerned, we believe that God Almighty will condemn the church organizations which fail to keep the faith, without any of our interference, regardless of creed or color." [95a]Lila and Joseph were certainly patriotic, as their lodge memberships demonstrated, but Lila kept her distance and her church's distance from the Klan and their exclusions. As KKK started another class July 31, 1923, "it is claimed

---

[94] Saunders, Ernest W. *Searching the Scriptures, a History of Biblical Literature, 1880-1980*, Scholars Press, Chico, Cal., 1982, p.3, 21
[95] Claude Thompson confession to me, *Interview*, 1985
[95a] *NE Press*, July 12, 1923, Addison Moore saw through the KKK subterfuge.

that there are over one hundred members in or near New Egypt at the present time." [96]

Klan members were elected as Ocean County Sheriff, as Ocean County Surrogate and to other NJ offices in the 1920's. Nearly 5000 Protestants gathered at Point Pleasant June 2, 1923 to hear the Great Titan and the Great Dragon of the KKK. Two hundred reporters covered the event that concluded with fireworks and the burning of an eighty-foot cross. Many ex-military men attended and didn't try to hide their identity. The Klan claimed to be five million strong nationally, plus the Royal Riders of the Red Robe (the acceptable naturalized citizens) and the Ladies of the Invisible Empire. They opposed the mixing of the races and fought to keep America 'clean.' This was code language; the KKK lynched a black man on the average of every four days in the South, including July Perry and eight others, after voting on Election Day, November 2, 1920, outside Orlando, Florida. The Rosewood, Florida Massacre in 1923 saw a whole town, almost all Black, either killed or run out of town, on the excuse of a suspected rape. These were only a few of the KKK terrorizing activities, North and South in the 1920's.[97]

Meanwhile, South Jersey's African-American population, except for the military, mostly consisted of seasonal farm laborers, "unskilled" laborers and servants in towns and cities. They always suffered de facto segregation and sometimes suffered de jure segregation. From its inception in 1850, Ocean County had no slaves, only freed blacks numbering 140. In comparison, Monmouth County, bordering Ocean on the north, still had plantations and seventy-five slaves, the largest number of the NJ counties. During this period in Allentown, Monmouth County, nine miles to the north of New Egypt, freed blacks organized the African Methodist Episcopal Church, established a school for their children with a teacher from Philadelphia, formed a benevolent society, and purchased land for a

---

[96] *NE Press*, Aug. 2, 1923; Claude Thompson Interview, 1989

[97] *NE Press*, June 7,1923; *The Rise and Fall of Jim Crow, The Terrors of Racism, part 3, PBS-TV, WEDU-TV,* Oct. 15, 2002; *Associated Press,* 1920 Election Day riot, lynching remembered, *Bradenton,* FL, *Herald,* Nov. 4, 2002; *Democracy Now, WMNF-FM,* Tampa, Nov. 6, 2002

cemetery on Hamilton Street. One former slave, Richard Hendrickson, solicited donations to buy a street light for the center of town, spearheaded Allentown's installation of street lamps in 1871 and the contributions to keep them lighted, as he was their unpaid street lighter. Nationally, there was no African-American representation in the U.S. Congress from 1902 until the 1930's when Adam Clayton Powell was elected from Harlem. Almost all state legislatures, counties and local governments had no African-American representation during the first one-third of the twentieth century, either. Heavyweight prize fighting champion Jack Johnson was the only African American hero allowed on the national stage in this period. [98]

Lila was an advocate for those discriminated against, later helping open her lodges' memberships to Jewish residents. In one Grand Session of the OES there was discussion about changing a few words in the ritual that were anti-Semitic. It was defeated. Many Jewish people broke off and formed the Order of the Golden Link. Lila felt distraught. She had so many people who were friends, such as Abe and Jane Holder, who were Jewish. On a visit to the Thompson homestead, Abe, in the furniture business, noticed that the walk-in closet in Lila's bedroom had no door, only a curtain. Without her knowing it, Abe quietly measured the opening. One day he returned in a snowstorm; on top of his car, wrapped in a quilt, was a beautiful beveled mirrored glass door, top to bottom. Abe said, "Mrs. Thompson, I didn't want you dressing in this room, anybody like you, without being able to see yourself." Later when Lila became Grand Matron of the Eastern Star, she made Jane Holder one of her appointees. Against bigotry, Lila was broadminded and inclusive and people from all walks of life loved her. [99] The Klan was not an issue in Lila's campaign, 1923. However, a month after the General Election, in December 1923, when the Klan was responsible for burning numerous crosses in New Egypt at road intersections and on the lawn

---

[98] Hull, Ellis F., *A Brief History of Old Allentown, Monmouth County, New Jersey, 1987, p.4;* known for its inclusiveness, I felt privileged to graduate from Allentown High School, 1954. African American History and Heritage which I taught in Los Angeles, 1966-74

[99] Linda Fote *Interview* of Claude Thompson, 1983

of the New Egypt Catholic Church, (KKK called these terrorist acts "symbols of righteousness;")[100] Lila and other community leaders opposed their hateful actions. Confronting the Klan was an exemplary stand and probably cost her votes in the following election.

Into the 1960's, except for the military, the only African Americans in the New Egypt area were seasonal farm workers and servants. The prevailing mores were indicated by the annual minstrel shows in the Isis Theater, sponsored by the New Egypt Lion's Club, the town's service club, where Claude was the Interlocutor (white face) and all the rest of the men were whites in black face making racist jokes to raise money. Dad even sang in black face portraying Al Jolson, the early "talkies" movie star. In other forms, racism continues to today in New Jersey. [101]

SEXISM

Bias against women remained as a major issue in the campaigns. The resistances to the rise of women, which included voting and holding public office, were expressed directly in public discourse. One of Lila's male supporters wrote during the campaign of 1923: "It pains me to hear anyone say you should not be sent to the Legislature because you are a woman. We should not forget that our mothers, sisters, and wives are women. I have no time for the person, male or female, who will not recognize ability in a woman or who does not recognize ability in a woman or does not think women are fully competent to take a hand in public matters."[102] The image that women were not competent was what Lila battled against in every election, especially 1921, 1923, and 1925. On the other hand she was a part of the progressive Republican tide in the 1920's that eventually reshaped attitudes toward women in electoral politics and systems of political power in New Jersey. However, with Legislatures raising the

---

[100] Miller, Pauline S., p. 548

[101] *NE Press*, Dec. 17, 1923 and Jan. 19, 1950; my growing up experiences in the 1940's and 1950's

[102] *Interview* of Claude Thompson, Linda Fote. 1983 includes this *NJ Courier* letter to the editor, 1923

pay and benefits of their members and the executive branch, men have made greater efforts for the seats, and the numbers of women in 2001 from New Jersey in U.S. Congress, state Legislature and Governor's mansion had declined from the 1990's.[103] Then as now, the price of democracy is eternal vigilance and community action to secure rights for all excluded people.

"JOHN BARLEY CORN"

Another issue was Prohibition, in effect 1919—1933, the Eighteenth Amendment to the US Constitution. Lila strongly supported Prohibition, outlawing the manufacture and sale of alcoholic beverages.[103a] This was an important issue in the General Election of 1923 and the Primary Election of 1925, when her opponents were opposed to Prohibition and many of her constituents slipped off to the Pine Barrens for their jug of moonshine. [104] Lila, seeing the devastating affect on families and communities, also opposed gambling and all corruption. Her Christian faith informed her positions, even confronting husband Joseph and son Sewell for violating Prohibition and drinking too much. [105]

In the 1920's and 1930's, Assembly terms were one year, while NJ Senate terms were two years. Lila first ran for Assembly in 1921 in the Republican Primary, the first woman to run for electoral position in Ocean County, and was defeated by Ezra Parker. Even though "the world beat a path to her door in the tiny town of New Egypt" it was not enough for winning the election. Lila was ready to run in the next election, 1922, but the heads of the Republican Party

---

[103] Trenton State Capitol Tour, Jan. 2001; Governor Christine Whitman resigned to accept an administrative appointment in Washington, DC
[103a] Goodman, Paul & Gatell, Frank O., *USA, An American Record,* Vol.2, p.447
[104] "County Sends First Woman to Assembly," *New Jersey Courier*, Founder's Day Souvenir Section, June 20, 1974
[105] Claude Thompson *Letter*, Nov. 2, 1977

promised Lila that if Ezra Parker served one more year, he would not run in 1923, and the support for Lila would be there. [106]

Being "well qualified" was not enough for a candidate either to be endorsed for election by her political party, or to be assured that promises made by her party to her would be fulfilled in the campaign. Joseph Thompson was very aware of duplicities from the more than twenty years he served as Chief Telegrapher and Chief Republican Page in the US House of Representatives. Next, we will look at the nature of political campaigns and what Lila experienced for herself in 1923.

PRIMARY ELECTION CAMPAIGN, 1923

No one knows the extreme tensions and demands of a political campaign unless they have been involved in one. I have been involved in many, on specific issues, such as supporting farm workers' rights and civil rights. Issue campaigns are stressful, but not usually as much as electioneering for particular candidates. I was immersed in several campaigns: in 1968, supporting Blase Bonpane for the non-partisan Los Angeles City Council position; 1972, supporting Jack Schaeffer for Congress in Inglewood, CA; and most recently, 2002, supporting Charles McKenzie for Congress in Arcadia, Bradenton and Sarasota, Florida. Win or lose, partisan election campaigns are a torturous process. New Jersey, including 2002, breeds venomous campaigns. A sense of humor, faith, and common goals maintained Lila and Joseph through the quagmires.

Early in the 1923 campaign, Republican Party leaders abrogated their promises of support for Lila. At an April 20, 1923 Republican dinner in Lakewood, "Former Judge W. Howard Jeffrey [is the candidate] for Assembly…It is evident that the Republicans are divided in selecting of candidates and the primary election promises to be a very exciting time and may result in a Democratic victory for

---

[106] Claude Thompson Taped *Interview* with me, 1976

some of these offices." Lila and Joseph were in attendance and upset at her being bypassed for Assembly, after promises to the contrary. [107]

A "MERE WOMAN" TAKES ON "THE GANG"

On May 24, 1923 at the Ocean County Court House, Lila W. Thompson announced her candidacy for Assembly on the Republican ticket at the Republican County Committee. "It is reported that this move did not suit all members of the committee present. Former Judge W. Howard Jeffrey of Toms River will be Mrs. Thompson's opponent at the polls on Primary day. It is said that Mrs. Thompson was promised the nomination this year without opposition. It is evident that the politicians in Ocean County forgot their promises even among their own flock." [108] On September 20, 1923, five days before the election, the *New Egypt Press* reported, "Jeffrey, without a doubt is a member of the "gang" and is being opposed on these grounds, while Mrs. Thompson is a "mere woman" and because her husband has made his living from politics ever since he was old enough, she is receiving her share of opposition."[109]

What is "the gang" so often referred to? According to interviews and newspaper accounts of that time, "the gang" was made up of men of high rank in the Republican Party who never made a move without the approval of the one who handpicked them, the party boss, Senator Thomas A. Mathis, an astute politician born in New Gretna near Tuckerton, Little Egg Harbor Township, which was split off by Burlington County to Ocean, because Burlington did not want the Republicans. To increase his influence, Tom lived in Toms River. He supported gambling in Point Pleasant and other 'smart' political acts. Elizabeth Miers Morgan, as a child, sat in Tom Mathis lap and she reminisced, "he smelled of fine elegant cigars and soft wool clothes." Elizabeth testified, "If you were not on Tom Mathis' side, your goose was cooked." As Zane Gray acutely observed, "A man can

---

[107] *NE Press*, April 26. 1923, Addison Moore, a Democrat, Editor

[108] *NE Press*, May 31, 1923

[109] *NE Press*, Sept.20, 1923

hide a mean disposition, but his shoes are always in sight." Or as Jersey City Democratic boss, Frank Hague, when confronted with the accusation, "you broke the law!" stated in reply, "I am the law!" "Mathis, the man who controlled the destinies of Ocean County for half a century, ended his turbulent political career early Sunday morning [May 18, 1958] with a .38 caliber pistol, embroiled in a bridge construction scandal and suffering from terminal cancer."[110]

With so much harassment and false accusations from "the gang" Lila paid for a public statement that appeared on the front page of the *New Egypt Press*, five days before the election,

"Dear Editor: The attacks have been very bitter and unfair. They were entirely uncalled for, especially from Postmaster Hagaman whom I have always known.

> 'There is so much bad in the best of us,
> And so much good in the worst of us,
> It hardly behooves any of us,
> To talk about the rest of us.'

I was born in New Egypt and have lived there all my life. Many people in the town have known me since my birth. My life is an open book; "Service for all" is my motto. I believe if "we would do unto others as we would have them do unto us" we would all be better citizens. There should be no sex discrimination insofar as public interests and responsibilities are concerned.

I ask the voters to think it over and I sincerely hope they will decide for the best. THEY HAVE THE LAST SAY. If they decide to place their trust in me I shall not disappoint them.
Very Sincerely, Mrs. Lila W. Thompson"[111]

---

[110] *New Jersey Courier*, May 22, 1958, Mathis Obituary reported the controversy regarding Mathis in the construction of a bridge and ill health. Elizabeth Miers Morgan *Interview*, in her living room, Forked River, June, 1998
[111] *NE Press*, Sept.20, 1923

In her campaign for New Jersey Assembly, 1923, Lila drove throughout Ocean County seeking votes. In practically all her campaigning, she drove herself, sometimes alone. One morning she stopped at a German-American's dairy farm in the Pinelands to ask for his vote. She told him she grew up on a dairy farm. In the barn, he asked her to sit down on the milking stool. Lila was a little uneasy, for it had been many years since she had done farm chores like milking. Without hesitation, she grasped the udder of the cow and rich full streams of milk flowed into the farmer's bucket. "I vote for you," smiled the German farmer. It was with this kind of persistence, drawing on her background and being friendly with everyone, that Lila won the primary election.[112]

RESULTS OF THE PRIMARY

Lila won the Republican Primary by 595 votes (3328 to 2733) over Judge W. Howard Jeffrey (Also, James McMurray received 281, & William E. Pharo 357 votes). She was the first woman to win nomination for any electoral position in the county. By comparison of pluralities in the Primary, in the three races—all males, one for Ocean County Surrogate, Clinton Fogg received 3223 votes, less than Lila, and the other for Ocean County Freeholder, William Butler received 3746 votes, more than Lila. [113] Claude Thompson reported that the Democrats at first had no candidate for the Assembly and invited Judge Jeffrey to oppose Lila in the General Election. He declined their invitation, saying, "No, Lila beat me fair and square in the Primary."[114] The Democratic opponent became James E. Lillie, former artillery lieutenant in Verdun, France, WWI and Oldsmobile Co. president in Toms River, who had lost to Ezra Parker in the 1922 Assembly election. At the time, New Egypt was on a par with Toms River as important centers of Ocean County, so there was competition

---

[112] Repeated in several Claude Thompson *Interviews* to me, 1976, 1978, 1986
[113] *New Jersey Courier*, Sept. 28, 1923, Toms River
[114] Claude Thompson *Interview*, 1976

between the two towns for having a dominant sway in the affairs of the county.[115]

Lila wrote a

"LETTER OF THANKS."

I wish to convey my sincere thanks to the Citizens of Ocean County who gave such an expression of confidence through their votes on September 25th. I promise in return to never betray that trust…To all my loyal supporters I am taking this means of publicly expressing my appreciation for their hearty co-operation and wonderful work. It occurs to me that now is the time to forget all party differences, put our shoulders to the wheel and roll up a sweeping majority for the whole Republican ticket. Again assuring you of my appreciation, I am Very Sincerely Yours, Lila W. Thompson"[116]

This thank you was particularly important for its conciliatory tone and call for Republican unity.

GENERAL ELECTION CAMPAIGN, 1923

The General Election campaign began immediately after the Primary. The editor of the *Lakewood Free Press* in a Democratic stronghold wrote: "Mrs. Lila W. Thompson who heads the ticket as candidate for the Assembly, is a resident of New Egypt. The *Free Press* editor was recently talking to a prominent Trenton man who was decidedly interested in Ocean County politics this year, who stated that Mrs. Thompson was just the type needed in Trenton. He was of the opinion that many typical politicians would oppose Mrs. Thompson because of the fact that they were afraid of getting a few such women in Trenton. Mrs. Thompson's ability is well known to

---

[115] *NE Press*, Sept. 27, 1923
[116] *NE Press*, Oct. 4, 1923

Ocean County and she would make an efficient member of the Assembly."[117]

The *Lakewood Free Press* endorsement of Lila was printed beside a full column of biography for opponent James Lillie in the *New Egypt Press*. Lila did not need her biography, for everyone in New Egypt knew and respected her.[118]

In the *New Jersey Courier*, not a Sen. Tom Mathis dominated paper, the editor wrote: "Mrs. Thompson I have known for a quarter century. She has been a good mother and a good citizen. She comes from one of the most respected families in Plumsted Township, being the daughter of the late Theodore Robbins. She knows the State from one end to the other and is herself widely known. Ocean County will be well represented in intelligence and moral worth by Mrs. Thompson."[119]

The *New Egypt Press*, which had not endorsed a candidate for Assembly in the Republican Primary earlier in 1923, printed:

"OUR OPINION OF MRS. LILA W. THOMPSON."

Mrs. Lila W. Thompson, the Republican candidate for the Assembly is making a thorough campaign throughout Ocean County. Mrs. Thompson is a wonderful woman, having served as national head of many of the fraternal societies of America. She has traveled in almost every state in the union. She has and still holds many offices of trust among these societies. She is a daughter of the late Mr. & Mrs. Theodore Robbins, one of the largest and most respected families in the county. She has always been a resident of Plumsted Township and the writer was one of her schoolmates in the old red schoolhouse at Archertown. If there is a nicer, cleaner and better

---

[117] *NE Press*, reprinted from the *Democratic Lakewood Free Press*, Oct. 18, 1923

[118] *NE Press*, Oct. 18, 1923

[119] *NE Press* reprinted NJ Courier endorsement of Lila, Oct. 18, 1923

woman in the county than Mrs. Thompson she has deceived us. She never shirks her duty. She is just a plain, poor, honest woman who has worked hard for her education. Her political faith is from birthright and from this point you are all free to pass judgment. With a large majority, she won the nomination in the county over three male candidates.

These remarks are made by The Press from a "home-pride" standpoint and without the consent of Mrs. Thompson. The Press is for "home" first, last and all the time." (Written by Addison Moore, a Democrat and owner editor, *New Egypt Press.*) [120]

The ground swell of endorsements by most of Ocean County's major newspapers projected victory for Lila.

RESULTS OF THE GENERAL ELECTION, 1923

Thus, Lila won her first victory for NJ Assembly November 6, 1923, with 5459 votes to 3829 votes for Lillie, a majority of 1630, as the Republicans swept the Ocean County election. In other contests, John Ernest, incumbent, won for County Clerk, with a 2891-vote majority, Clinton Fogg won County Surrogate with a 3253-vote majority, and William Butler won County Freeholder with a 2307-vote majority. As in the 1923 Primary, Lila was the only woman candidate in Ocean Countywide contests. The majority vote for Lila was less than the men who won. This indicated the anti-woman bias, and yet she became the first Ocean County woman in elective office. [121]

The New York Times carried the news of her groundbreaking achievement as the first woman to represent an entire county in NJ. *The Times* had featured Ocean County in 1915 when it was the only county in NJ to vote for women's suffrage in that state election ballot.

---

[120] *NE Press* endorsement of Lila, Oct. 25, 1923; Addison Moore was perceptive and sometimes courageous, as in his earlier 1923 editorial against the KKK.

[121] *NE Press*, Nov. 8, 1923

It took five more years to pass nationally in 1920. *The Times* was very generous in its praise of Lila and her successful campaign. Obviously, it was not easy with the party leadership's opposition to a woman winning the election. * [122]

Lila wrote a

"CARD OF THANKS."

"To My Dear Friends and Neighbors:
    Words fail me in trying to express my appreciation for your loyal support during the campaign just closed…You have elected me to represent all the people…It is my earnest wish to be of service to all.

Again, thanking you,
Lila W. Thompson" [123]

---

[122] *The New York Times*, Oct. 23, 1915 and *Nov, 7, 1923
[123] *NE Press*, Nov. 15, 1923

Donald C. Thompson

CHAPTER SIX

ACTION IN THE GENERAL ASSEMBLY, 1924-25

"Turn, Turn, Turn. To everything there is a season and a time to every purpose under heaven: a time to be born and a time to die; a time to sow and a time to reap; a time to kill and a time to heal; a time to tear down and a time to build up; a time to weep and a time to laugh; a time to mourn and a time to dance; a time to cast away stones and a time to gather stones together; a time to embrace and a time to refrain from embracing...A time to love and...a time of peace, I swear it's not too late. Turn, Turn, Turn." (Ecclesiastes 3:1-5, 8, KJV) [124]

Chapter Six details Lila's struggles and accomplishments in the General Assembly, flavored by her integrity and marked by her becoming the first woman to have a powerful influence on the New Jersey Legislature. It concludes with the excruciating Election Campaign of 1925.

Let's take a thorough look at how Lila accomplished her priorities in the patriarchal Legislature. She was well respected by Democrats and Republicans in the NJ Assembly in 1924 and 1925, including Republican Assemblyman Harold Hoffman, who was later elected congressman and governor. She was sworn in Tuesday, January 8, 1924, as many state, county, and hometown friends joined her for the ceremony. There were many floral tributes to Lila [125] in the historic second oldest Statehouse in continuous use in USA. This was also the first Statehouse to be equipped with electricity (in 1892). Near the Delaware River in Trenton, its gold dome overshadows the

---

[124] *Holy Bible, King James Version,* Thomas Nelson, Nashville, 1994, as modified and sung by the Byrds in the album, *Turn, Turn, Turn*
[125] *NE Press,* Jan. 10, 1924

Statehouse Annex and the Hessian Headquarters beside it, which Gen. George Washington captured, Christmas, 1776. [123]

Lila ran for re-election to the Assembly and was unopposed in the Republican Primary, September 23, 1924. She completed her election victory against Walter S. Hendrickson, Democrat, winning easily, 6902 to 3702 votes, a 3200 vote majority, November 4, 1924.[127]

During Lila's two years in the Assembly, she served on six committees: Clergy, Highways, Social Welfare, Joint Social Welfare, Industrial School for Girls and State Reformatory for Women; and chaired three: the Clergy, State Reformatory for Women and Social Welfare Committees. In 1925, Clifford R. Powell, the Republican Assembly Speaker, appointed her chairperson of the latter. Then Lila appointed a page from New Egypt, Joseph H. Watson; and a clerk, former sheriff, Joseph H. Holman. Many people were especially excited that the previous Speaker had appointed her to the Highway Committee in 1924. This would greatly help with the needed road legislation, one of the major issues in the state. [128]

BUILD ROADS VERSUS NO MORE TAXES

On December 17, 1923, before the 1924 legislative session, the Good Roads Dinner at Dunkel's, New Egypt, hosted the major players: Board of Freeholders' Director Wm. Savage, & members Wm. Butler and Frank Holman; Sen. Tom Mathis and Assemblywoman Lila were all present and supportive of paving hard surfaced roads much needed in Ocean County, such as the Trenton to Lakewood road through New Egypt. A motion approved and added

---

[123] Trenton State Capitol Tour, Sept. 2000

[127] Smith, Cynthia H., *Ocean County Women in the Legislature: The Struggle for Equality in Representation,* p.14, *NJ Courier*, Sept. 26, 1924, Nov. 7, 1924

[128] *NE Press*, for 1925 Committees and appointments: Jan. 1, 1925; for 1924 Committees, Jan. 10, 1924; *Asbury Park Evening Press*, May 17, 1965

that the road from Main Street, New Egypt to the Burlington County line near Cookstown be paved.[129] Although these motions were not official actions, similar bills were presented in the state legislature or the county Board of Freeholders in 1924.

Priorities of Governor Silzer, 1924, were: roads, guaranteeing a plentiful supply of coal from Pennsylvania; with President Coolidge, enforcing Prohibition of alcohol and drugs; cooperating with New York (NY) Port Authority Commission in completing the tunnel under the Hudson, constructing more tunnels and bridges connecting NY and NJ, combating seashore pollution, promoting educational and other institutional projects, conservation of water and possibilities of the Delaware River for electrical power. Gov. Silzer ended his term with frustration at the "do nothing" legislature. [130]

The issue that made it difficult for NJ Legislators and Ocean County Freeholders to fulfill these priorities was substantial opposition to increased taxes: sales, income, real estate or otherwise. Almost every edition of the newspapers had an editorial, article or letter to the editor on the need to keep taxes low and/or reduce taxes. The vision for paved roads and building schools were among Lila's battles to gain funding against the no taxation people. [131] For example, Lila's first road bill lost 27-25, March 7, 1924, for the Bordentown-New Egypt-Lakewood road construction, but she persevered later. On the same Friday, Lila secured passage in both houses of Assembly Bill 439, calling for "the presentation by Board of Education to all graduates of grammar schools, a book containing the Constitution of the USA, the Declaration of Independence, and the Constitution of New Jersey." The *New Egypt Press* noted there were sufficient funds in the state board's budget to present them.[132]

The State Highway Commission indicated to the Ocean County Freeholders the possible building of the Lakewood to Toms

---

[129] *NE Press*, Dec. 20, 1923
[130] *NE Press*, Jan. 10, 1924 and Mar. 13, 1924
[131] *NE Press*, Feb. 19, 1925
[132] *NE Press*, Mar. 13, 1924

River road, reversing its past decision and diverting that money for the Hudson Tunnel and Delaware River Bridge approaches. As a member of the Assembly Highway Committee, Lila sponsored and secured the passage of Assembly Bill 18 in the 1925 session, extending Route 7, now US Route 9, from Adelphia over 'Old Stage Road' through Lakewood. Meanwhile, the Ocean County Freeholders approved paving six miles of the most used part of the New Egypt-Lakewood Road, closest to New Egypt and the New Egypt Main Street to Burlington County near Cookstown road. Joseph Thompson was present on March 18, 1924, for the vote.[133]

Lila sponsored and secured passage of Assembly Bill 4 to clarify Chapter 236 Laws of 1924 governing the Ocean County Prosecutor's Salary, so s/he could have a living wage. In Assembly Bill 171, she renewed the presentation of a copy of the Declaration of Independence, US Constitution and NJ Constitution to each pupil graduating from grammar school. She was the deciding vote in the Assembly's passage of a bill for daily Bible reading of five verses of the Old Testament, as well as five verses from the New Testament, in each elementary school class. This continued with the Lord's Prayer in NJ schools until the 1960's USA Supreme Court's decision prohibited both in response to Madeline Murray O'Hair's legal suit.[134]

STANDING WITH INTEGRITY

It was clear from the outset that Lila was not going to be told by others what to do and seemed to be leading the other women Assembly members in that direction. Lila was said to be the first woman to have significant impact on the NJ Legislature. For example, in February 1924, Lila reacted with hostility to the bossism of Mrs. Felckert, vice-president of the Republican State Committee. Felckert commanded Lila to support the bill to remove the NJ Commissioner of Education from the Governor's control and put the Commissioner

---

[133] *NE Press*, Mar. 20, 1924

[134] *NJ Legislative Index*, 1925, NJ Historical Library, secured Mar. 7. 1989; Linda Fote *Interview* of Claude Thompson

under the control of the State Board of Education. Lila refused in no uncertain terms, saying; "the people of Ocean County had elected her and she was responsible for her actions to them and that the vice-chairman of the state committee could not threaten her with impunity." Today, we would say, "She set her boundaries!" The *New Egypt Press* approved, entitling the article: "Mrs. Thompson Making Good At Trenton."[135]

The same realism pervaded her relations with men. She did not dislike men; neither was she sentimental over them. She liked to laugh and enjoyed a good joke, but men could not intimidate her. She never drank nor smoked. In the Assembly, when they went into caucus somebody offered her a drink. Lila responded, "I don't drink!" Another legislator offered her a cigarette. "I don't smoke," she said. One wise guy said, "Well, if you're in the legislature very long, you'll drink and smoke." Lila persisted, "If I'm in the legislature one hundred years, I won't drink or smoke." She set her limits from the outset, but she was no prude. Joseph and Sewell both smoked and drank. She did not make herself obnoxious, but others could not shake her integrity.[136]

A KEEN OBSERVER

In navigating political structures, Lila listened and observed people well on all levels of life, including the president. President Warren Harding, Republican, died from illness (diagnosed as apoplexy; a stroke) in office, August 2, 1923, and the entire nation greatly mourned his death. This happened during Lila's first successful election campaign. Vice President Calvin Coolidge became president and was re-elected in 1924. Coolidge was quirky and demanding. For example, he had his blood pressure checked the same time nightly before supper. If Dr. Joel Thompson Boone, Coolidge's physician, were a moment late, he was greeted by a scowl and a

---

[135] *NE Press*, Feb. 5. 1924
[136] Linda Fote *Interview* with Claude Thompson; Rev. F. Elwood Perkins *Remarks*

reprimand. On the other hand, Mrs. Coolidge, who was in poor health, was a fine woman almost always greeting Dr. Boone with a smile. The great shock to the Coolidge family was, through an infected blister, Calvin Coolidge, Jr. contracted blood poisoning with high fever and, with no miracle drugs, Calvin, Jr. died on July 7, 1924. When President and Mrs. Coolidge realized the battle to save their son was lost, they gazed at him in death, rose silently, expressed gratitude to all who attended Jr. and left quickly returning to the White House. Their fortitude and self-control, restraining their grief, were evident throughout the vigil and realization of Jr.'s death. In contrast, Dr. Boone was so grief stricken, he never recovered from the death of Jr. Lila was well aware of how these events and the feelings and other characteristics of the people involved affected everyone in the country, especially those involved in politics.[137]

In addition, Lila was listened to because she did her homework. She always read proposed legislation ahead of time. At home she used the dining room table as her desk and worked until one or two in the morning on preparations. She chided legislators in the newspapers for not reading the bills considered by the legislature. She maintained, "They serve the party best who serve the people best." Lila was always ready and willing to serve the people, fairly, forcefully, and faithfully. "No night was too dark, no road too long and no day too stormy."[138]

Another priority was adequate hospital care for the public. Lila, as a member of the Board of Managers of the Paul Kimball Hospital, a public hospital in Lakewood, and as a member of the Assembly, exerted great influence on the public to add to and improve the hospital and its care for all people. She supported fund raising drives that increased the hospital's efforts and enabled it to survive in the lean times.[139]

---

[137] Heller, Milton F., Jr., *The President's Doctor- An Insider's View of Three First Families,* Vantage Press, NYC, 2000, pp.66-70, 73-83; Dr. Joel Thompson Boone was a native of St. Clair, PA.

[138] Bishop Library, Toms River, Ocean County Public Library historical files, visited 1998

[139] *NE Press*, Feb. 12 1924, Feb. 19, 1924

IN THE MIDST OF THE LEGISLATIVE SESSION: CAMPAIGN 1925, NOT A FAIR FIGHT

ROUND ONE

The Democratic Minority Leader of the Assembly, Morris "Leo" Barrison, of Hudson County, later a New Jersey Supreme Court Justice, came to Lila and said, "If you are ever in a tight spot and need the votes to pass legislation, come to me and I will find the votes." Leo and Lila differed in gender, political parties, ethics, values, and priority issues, but they worked together. How is this possible? An end of the twentieth century example of political opposites working together were Washington D.C. Democrat Congresswoman with no vote, Eleanor Holmes Norton, and GA Republican Speaker of the House, Newt Gingrich. He gave her the majorities needed to secure the legislation Eleanor knew the District of Columbia needed, according to her radio interview in 2003.

That happened during the 1925 session for Lila. "The bill in question was the construction of a bridge in Pine Bluff, a section in which Mrs. Thompson…is said to be particularly strong." Tom Mathis, the Ocean County boss, a Republican, introduced the bridge bill in the New Jersey Senate, and Lila introduced it in the Assembly. When Mathis anticipated a tight race with Lila in the Republican Primary for the Senate post that year, he withdrew his support in the Assembly from the bill he had introduced. It was his effort to discredit Lila's ability to pass legislation. To Lila's chagrin, the bridge bill lost on the first vote in the Assembly. She went to Leo Barrison, the Democratic leader and revealed, "Tom Mathis is attempting to embarrass me by forcing key Republicans not to vote for the bridge bill; we are five or six votes short of approving it." Leo heard her concern: "I cannot vote for your bridge bill, but you will have the needed eight votes for passage." Mr. Barrison fulfilled his promise:

the needed votes for a majority came from the Democrats and the bridge bill passed in the Assembly on the second attempt.[140]

When interviewed, Mathis denied he had withdrawn his support, but everyone knew his duplicity. When the Assembly passed and Governor Edge signed the bridge bill, Tom Mathis almost had a heart attack at Lila's effectiveness.[141] The Assembly passage underlined Lila's credibility, stateswomanship and effectiveness in organizing, especially in the political pressure cooker of campaign opposition by the party boss. It also underlined why she took the great risk of running for state Senate against the party boss. She knew how important it was to pass much needed legislation and oppose political deception and bossism.

ROUND TWO

Mathis' behind the scenes influence within the 1925 Gov. Edge's organization netted him the chair of the prestigious Senate Appropriations Committee. Later, Mathis' "gang" and/or Edge's organization were behind the pressure that urged the State Institutions & Agencies Commissioner Burdette G. Lewis, to have Lila's husband and companion on evening campaign stops transferred in his job assignment to the north: not North Jersey, but to Boston; Albany, NY; and New York City, far out of New Jersey. Mr. Thompson blew the whistle on this political behind the scenes campaign chicanery. It not only prevented Joseph from driving for or riding with Lila, but from being home in order to vote in this fateful election. To make matters worse, Tom Mathis even paid for ads in the last editions of the county's many newspapers published before the election for Senate in 1925, blaming the Thompsons for creating the story of the transfer and "mudslinging from New Egypt."[142]

---

[140] *NE Press*, Mar. 19, 1925 and Claude Thompson *Interview* with me, Nov. 1976

[141] Ibid

[142] *NE Press*, June 18, 1925

Lila did not have time to refute these preposterous allegations in print before the election. Mathis again denied that he was the "complainant" about Joseph Thompson. Instead, he had Lewis lead the condemnation of Joseph, who was a long time responsible employee. On Wednesday, after the Tuesday, June 23 Primary Election, Joseph was dismissed from his $4,000. a year post as Chief Inspector of Institutions and Agencies. Completing this action, Mathis and his cohorts placed vociferous blame on the Thompsons for creating the story and Joseph bringing about the transfer himself![143]

Earlier, Lila had pursued the charge that Mathis made the complaint against Joseph.

"While at first this action of my opponent was very discouraging to me, yet so many real friends have risen to take up the fight, that I am now more determined than ever, with Divine help, to fight this battle to the finish…And I wish to assure the good citizens of Ocean County, at whose urgent request I entered the fight, that I will not withdraw, though there be arrayed against me-and them-practically every big organized force of evil in the county, bootlegger, every big gambler, and all. I am forced to make this statement 'lest the silence of self-respect be misunderstood'…The people of the county will have the final say at the primary."[144]

What a courageous woman. She fought to the finish!

ROUND THREE

A final factor in the contest was apparent. Earlier in the 1925 legislative session, Mathis and his "gang," and the governor's organization arranged for the Primary Elections in New Jersey to be shifted in date from the end of September to the end of June, with the excuse that it gave the primary winners more time to campaign for the

---

[143] *NE Press*, June 4, 18, 25, 1925; *Lakewood Citizen*, June 5, 19, 26, 1925; and Claude Thompson *Interview* with me, 1976
[144] *Lakewood Citizen*, June 5, 1925

General Election. It did that, but the real reason was to give challengers within the same party less opportunity to garner much needed support versus the incumbents, who already had massive support. Facing all the accusations and election 'tactics', this abrupt change in date put Lila in a real bind in the January to June 1925 campaign for Republican candidate for State Senate, especially since much of that time Lila was fulfilling her responsibilities in the Assembly.[145]

"Show me the money" could have originated in 1925. Add the difference between rich powerful party boss and poor (in money) Assembly member, Lila, to the equation. She spent less than $5,000. on her campaign. Mathis spent at least $250,000. (equivalent to $1 million or more in the year 2002) in writing and producing a silent film about how great a legislator he was, and all the contributions he had made, including taking credit for the passage of the bridge bill that he had opposed in the Assembly in 1925. The Mathis film appeared in every town in Ocean County during the primary campaign for Senate; all had movie theaters at that time and all moviegoers were exposed to Mathis' expensive propaganda film.[146]

Why this vicious campaigning by the party boss? Mathis made a vow in 1910 when he lost the race for State Senator by eighty-one votes that he would never lose an election again. After the 1910 vote tally was completed, the electioneers mysteriously produced enough votes for Mathis to win. The NJ judge threw out the eighty-one votes that came in late and Tom had to sit those three years outside the legislature. In 1925 Mathis pulled in every person and organization for which he had ever done favors, or to whom he promised favors, to vote against Lila.[147]

---

[145] *NE Press*, June 14, 1925 shows the results.

[146] Claude Thompson *Interview*, 1976

[147] Ibid and *NJ Courier*, Toms River, May 22, 1958: Tom Mathis Obituary

HER LAST ROUND

Thus, Lila lost the 1925 election to Tom Mathis by 609 votes of 8011 cast. She never ran for public office again. Quotes abound on Mathis' bossism of Ocean County for 50 years, 1908-1958. Some writers criticize Lila for a major blunder in running for the Senate against the party boss. The fact is that no woman was elected from any county to the NJ Senate, until Mildred Barry Hughes was elected in 1966, a Democrat from Union County. No woman has ever been elected to the NJ Senate from Ocean County. Sexism still inhabits election booths and legislative halls. [148] Lila showed great vision and courage in her Senate bid.

In spite of the criticism, Lila was designated: "Mother of the Assembly," an honor not extended before or after. The importance of the mothering quality conveyed by Lila cannot be underestimated, as indicated by women's fashions of that era. A Metropolitan Museum of Art, New York City, special exhibit December 2001, showed how society mandated contortions of the female body through the ages; bound feet were the worst manipulation. The USA fashion of the 1910's and 1920's highlighted the 'pigeon breast' look in women. Women wore 'one breast bras' that emphasized their highly valued motherhood quality.[149]

Lila completed her second and final legislative term in 1925, shortly before the Primary Election. A week after she lost the election, Lila was seriously injured in an auto accident. She had just pulled up her thick coat collar before the accident or the glass shards from the windshield would have surely killed her. Meanwhile, Joseph was barely scratched when their car turned over. The auto accident was a harbinger of Lila's future.[150]

---

[148] *New Jersey Women in the Legislature*, 1995, p. 47; *Ocean County Women in the Legislature*, 1998, p. 1-38.

[149] Metropolitan Museum of Art. NYC, visit Dec. 10, 2001 in a Special Exhibit showing through the ages, contortions of the female body

[150] *NE Press*, June 18, 1925; Tom Mathis Obituaries, May 18-22, 1958; *NJ Legislature Index*, 1925 session.

Donald C. Thompson

CHAPTER SEVEN

RISING FROM THE ASHES

"As far as we are concerned, we do not want to stand in anyone's way, nor do we wish to bring discredit on the service God has given us. Indeed, we want to prove ourselves genuine servants of God, whatever we have to go through...Our sole defense, our only weapon is a life of integrity, whether we meet honor or dishonor, praise or blame. Called 'imposters,' we must be true; called 'nobodies,' we must be in the public eye. Never far from death, but here we are alive! Always "going through it," but never "going under." We know sorrow, yet our joy is inextinguishable. We have nothing to bless ourselves with, yet we bless many others with true riches." (II Corinthians 6: 3-4.8-10)[151]

Like the phoenix, Lila and Joseph rose from the ashes of Lila's defeat in 1925. Chapter Seven depicts the eight years of extremely significant work that followed. It concludes with reflections on her life after her untimely death.

"GIVE ME YOUR TIRED, YOUR POOR"

Among her finest achievements, Lila spent the rest of her life, 1925-1933, helping the poor and needy, continuing her work directing the Daughters of America Orphans Department and through being the first Director of the Old Age Assistance Bureau, appointed January 21, 1932, which later became the Welfare Department of Ocean County. She was paid $30. a month. Her selection was based on her experience chairing the Social Welfare Committee in the Assembly and directing the D of A Orphans' Fund, which she managed from October 22, 1915, until her death.

---

[151] *The New Testament in Four Versions, J.B. Phillips Modern English Version*, p.557, 559

Her Old Age Assistance directorship occurred when the Great Depression hit Ocean County the hardest, 1932-33. She had extremely limited resources from her financially strapped agency and county, with Congress denying the situation. In 1932 John Inman, New Egypt postmaster, visited Washington, DC and interviewed US Senator Barbour and Third District Congressman, William Sutphin, Republicans from New Jersey. Inman quipped, "They don't seem to know anything about *depression* down here"[in Washington.] [152]

FIGHTING FOR THE UNDERDOG

Lila had the ability to take meager resources and stretch them into positive results beyond human comprehension. It's the ability to "make do", the Jesus loaves and fishes story that takes a scanty amount of food and feeds a multitude, that she learned on the farm. Both Lila and Joseph fought for the underdog, the oppressed, and the disadvantaged. Leaders in the Klan criticized them: "They interfere with justice too much." The "interference with justice" was trying to help poor people who couldn't afford an attorney because they had gotten into some difficulty where they weren't actually bad, but had gotten on the wrong track. Lila or Joseph would testify for them in court.[153]

She was central in the health care efforts that included keeping Paul Kimball Hospital in Lakewood from closing. The hospital continued open when Lila, a Board member, secured John D. Rockefeller matching grants for every $1,000. raised. She helped influence doctors to settle in Ocean County, such as Dr. J. Edwin Obert in New Egypt in 1930.[154] Knowing the importance of public libraries and the availability to read free books, she served on the Ocean County Library Commission from 1928 until her death. As a volunteer, she was the first chair of the Commission and raised the

---

[152] *NE Press*, April 14, 1932

[153] Claude Thompson material in *My Autobiography*, 1951; Linda Fote *Interview*

154 Six years later he was the doctor who delivered me from my Mother Irene's womb.

money that put the Free Library into operation in its first location, a house in Toms River. The Board of Freeholders had appropriated no funding during the Great Depression. She had been selected for another term. Lila knew the importance of history and continued her work in the New Jersey and Ocean County Historical Societies, that she had been instrumental in starting. [155]

JOSEPH IN THE LEGISLATURE

Lila supported husband Joseph in his elections and service in the NJ Assembly, 1930-31. They were the first husband and wife team in NJ politics. Joseph was able to complete legislative efforts his wife had begun in the Assembly: constructing roads and attracting businesses to Ocean County, such as the Women's Apparel Factory moving into the first floor of the old school building in New Egypt, and helping them survive. WWI veterans' pensions and other old age pensions and assistance were a major part of this dedicated couple's service to the people. However, like Lila, Joseph met defeat in the State Senate campaign against young attorney Percy Camp, handpicked by Tom Mathis in 1933. The deciding votes arrived with names from the Beachwood Cemetery in the very close election of 1933 and showed the extent to which the party boss would go to win elections, submitting the votes of dead people for his candidate. [156]

Joseph and Lila were among the few natives of Ocean County who had the wisdom to see the perversity of the Republican Ocean County party boss system and the courage to publicly oppose Tom Mathis and his "gang." Willa Cather in her book, *A Lost Lady* (1923) pits the noble, creative producer of unity of humans and nature into caring communities, the servant of the people, against the threat by the ugly, venal, amoral exploiter/villain who sells as easy and pleasant distractions what others make, intent only on minimizing risks and

---

[155] *NE Press*, July 25 monthly through Dec. 1, 1977, New Egypt Historical Society, led by Dayton Hopkins, extolled Lila's and others' contributions.
[156] Claude Thompson told this vignette with a cynical laugh, *Interviews* 1951, 1976, 1986

maximizing profits.[157] The Thompsons paid high prices for following their sense of God's calling for them in public service in opposing the exploiter/boss Cather described. They were true "humanitarians." Ann Ryan, 91, of New Egypt noted: "I remember Lila very well. She was well known for her honesty. I believe she always spoke the truth." [158]

Lila maintained her local, state and national leadership in the lodge and local church. Rev. F. Elwood Perkins, her Methodist pastor in New Egypt from April 2, 1931, when he arrived from Princeton Seminary and Graduate School, until the end of her life, testified to her effectiveness as the first woman chair of the Board of Stewards, the governing board of the church, and personal mentor to the Perkins family.[159]

As noted, Lila was Director of the Orphans' Department, D of A. In 1924, after serving her first term in the Assembly, Joseph and she made a trip to the Springfield, Ohio orphanage. Two of the children they met that day made a profound impression on them. Blodwyn (Winnie) Childers, age nine, and her little brother, Wilbur Levi Childers, age six. They were from Jackson, Ohio, where their father had died from influenza and pneumonia, leaving their mother to raise Winnie and Wilbur. Mrs. Childers worked for the Kelley family in Columbus for two years, taking care of the numerous Kelley children and her own two, as well as housekeeping.

When their mother became ill with pneumonia and died, Winnie and Wilbur were put into the orphanage. Lila found them there and her heart was touched. Part of her responsibility directing the Orphans' Department was placing orphans in homes. For that purpose, Lila and Joseph took Winnie and Wilbur to New Egypt with them. Lila found a fine home in Dunellen, where Winnie was placed with the Sauter family.

---

[157] Hoffman, Frederick J., *The 20's American Writing in the Postwar Decade*", p.182-183

[158] Claude Thompson from Lila & Joseph's Obituaries, to me 1951; Ann Rockhill Ryan, NE Historical Society, June 26, 2002

[159] Rev. F. Elwood Perkins, *Remarks* in May 1975 & 1976 at Route 9 Memorial Service

Lila then pursued the possibility of placing Wilbur with a New Egypt farm family, who had received other orphans. Lila left Wilbur in the car when they reached the farm, saying, "Stay inside the car until I return in a few minutes." Lila went inside, met the family and saw the conditions. She returned to the car and told Wilbur, "You are not staying here; you are coming home with me." When Wilbur was older, Lila explained to him, "I saw the farm family treating its children like slaves in the field, and I would not let you be treated that way." I'm sure she did what she could to help those children, also.[160]

Lila raised Wilbur Childers from his age six until her untimely death, in what would be called today, 'foster care'. Kids teased, "Where did you come from?" Wilbur replied with a smile, "Sears and Roebuck!" Questioners liked him for his spunk, sense of humor and kind personality, calling him "Searsy." In New Egypt Elementary School, in Miss Myrtle Moore's fourth grade class play, Wilbur portrayed George Washington and Carolyn Lear was Betsy Ross. They, with all the other 1931 graduates of New Egypt Elementary School, entered Allentown High School, September 9, 1931. Lila brought forth his positive self-identity and youthful enthusiasm in New Egypt. And she saw that Wilbur's older sister was cared for beginning at age nine.[161]

Mae Childers, Wilbur's widow, attested that he always commented, "I could not have had a better mother than Lila." He cited the example of not being able to play outside on Sundays, between the morning and evening church services at the Methodist Episcopal Church. Wilbur spent that time reading, swinging on the front porch swing, working crossword puzzles, and playing board games with his friends. He learned to love reading and working crossword puzzles, reading every opportunity he had, until macular degeneration deprived him of his sight in his last years. Wilbur also maintained, "There could not have been a better place to grow up than the town of New Egypt; family and neighbors always knew what was

---

[160] Mae Childers phone call, Oct. 1, 2002
[161] *NE Press*, Sept. 3, 1931; Carolyn Lear in discussion, NE Historical Society, June 26, 2002

going on. You couldn't do something wrong without word coming home."[162] I can attest to that!

I was haunted by the question, "Why didn't Lila officially adopt Wilbur?" Mae answered, "Lila was in the process of officially adopting Wilbur when she died!" Joseph did not want to adopt alone. Claude and Irene continued the raising of Wilbur and received the official state document, having custody of him from the time of Lila's death until he "became of age." Wilbur embraced Lila, calling her, "Mother," and could not praise her enough for how she raised him and for the wonderful person she was. [163]

Earlier that year, July 9, 1931, Lila purchased and thoroughly renovated with $3,000. of her own money, a home beside the Thompson homestead on the Lakewood Road side, into a funeral home for Claude to direct. Claude had recently completed embalming school in Philadelphia. Returning home from school late at night, he escaped serious injury in an auto accident, when he fell asleep driving on Camp Dix Road. He was also experiencing grief at the loss of a close friend and baseball teammate in the spring of 1931. Claude re-evaluated his life.

---

[162] Mae Childers phone call, Oct. 21, 2002
[163] Ibid

He proposed to Irene DeCou, one of the popular girls of Pemberton, whom Dad had been dating since 1926. According to her scrapbooks and relative's accounts, "she was fun loving and the life of the party." Irene, her seven sisters and mother, Emma, persevered after father Eber DeCou, a prominent mill operator, died in 1912. Claude and Irene married on July 23, 1931 at the Pemberton Methodist Episcopal Church with Rev. George Taylor officiating. Claude, who began as a singer, dancer and magician, was settling down at age 25. Lila had prayed that he would become a Methodist minister, but now accepted funeral directing combined with work at the New Egypt post office as a positive path for Claude. [164]

The Thompson's oldest son, Sewell, married Jennie Trimmer of Trenton, August 29, 1931, his third wife, and successfully pursued his business career in Vincentown. He had begun his business career as a teenager owning and operating poolrooms and bowling alleys, which he sold at age twenty-one. [165]

LILA'S UNTIMELY DEATH

The world seemed to stop when Lila died tragically on Monday, April 3, 1933. This dedicated woman was driving home from her Toms River office to New Egypt. On the Lakewood Road in Cassville, she allegedly fell asleep from exhaustion due to her work. Some accounts speculated she had a heart attack. The car went across the road and struck a tree. Lila was killed when she "was thrown partly through the Buick's windshield and the glass cut her throat." [166] This was before safety glass. Having given her life completely for others, her family and friends were devastated at the news of her "untimely death." It is a deep irony that one of Lila's primary concerns as a pioneer in the legislature was directing and supporting

---

[164] *NE Press*, July 9 and 30, 1931

[165] Lila's *Family Bible*. Sewell was interred in Vincentown until Claude brought his remains to be beside Lila, Joseph, and Carlton's in Jacobstown; *NE Press*, Oct. 23, 1914

[166] *Associated Press Release*, Cassville, April 4, 1933

NJ highway construction, for which she was posthumously memorialized. On one of those roads she met her death.

She was mourned at her funeral in the greatest outpouring of affection, through attendance and flowers, in Ocean County history. The funeral was on a rainy, dreary April 8, 1933 Saturday, in the New Egypt Methodist Episcopal Church that she loved so much. Jesus seemed to be weeping, according to one living witness. Her pastor, F. Elwood Perkins, led the overflow crowd of mourners in celebrating her life and ongoing spirit: "The Lord is my shepherd, I shall not want. He maketh me to lie down in green pastures; he leadeth me beside still waters. He restoreth my soul; he leadeth me in the paths of righteousness for his name's sake. Yea, though I walk through the valley of the shadow of death, I will fear no evil, for thou art with me; thy rod and thy staff they comfort me. Thou preparest a table before me in the presence of mine enemies; thou anointest my head with oil; my cup runneth over. Surely, goodness and mercy shall follow me all the days of my life; and I will dwell in the house of the Lord forever." After the services, flowers covered the long porch of the Thompson homestead and the gravesite, for all to see how she was revered.[167]

REFLECTIONS

Perkins reflected forty-two years later on the significance of Lila at the rededication of the plaque and monument to her on Route 9 at Adelphia Road: "Mother Thompson was a good neighbor and a second mother to the young married couple, our infant son and little daughter in the parsonage. Our little girl would run across the way just as though the home of the Thompson's were her own. Goodies were often brought across the street, appreciated all the more because the times were hard. The local bank closed. [We were provided for] because our parishioners were [warmhearted] farmers.

---

[167] Psalm 23, *The Holy Bible, King James Version,* Thomas Nelson Publisher, *p.*810; Elizabeth Miers Morgan Interview, June, 1998

"I recall her state-wide leadership in the beneficial work of the lodges, especially as the Grand Matron of the Eastern Star…She gave leadership in the purchase[168]and development of the first Home for the Elderly of [OES] in the lovely valleys of Far Hills near Bernardsville [formerly the castle-like home of one of the Childs family, known for their restaurant chain]. It was my privilege to accompany her once a month to conduct a devotional service for her friends at 'The Home.' It gave me an opportunity…to hold conversation with an interesting couple upon many subjects…I had become quite close to the Thompsons.

"When meeting people who have accomplished something for God and others,…I've tried to discover the secret and meaning of the personal dedication which is always associated with the individual's life and work. For Lila Thompson the deep motivation was her Christian love of people, her friendship for all persons she met, and her open outgoing heart of good-will and helpfulness. Out of this heart and will she had vision to see needs that must be met for the sake of people. I am sure she knew that God loves people and that as a Christian it was a privilege for her to love and serve God's children.

"The supporting strength of her life was prayer and the worship [life] of the congregation…unseen to the casual eye but very real - like the hidden supports of a bridge…In those days there were evening services. Rarely did she miss…Her favorite gospel song was "The Beautiful Garden of Prayer." I remember well being at a dinner gathering with her when an editor from Lakewood paid tribute to her and quoted the lines:

> " 'It is the human touch in this world that counts,
> The touch of your hand and mine.
> That means far more to the fainting heart
> Than shelter or bread or wine,
> For shelter is gone when the night is o'er,

---

[168] Perkins, Rev. F. Elwood, *Remarks* delivered at Route 9 Lila W. Thompson Memorial Rededications, May 18, 1975 & May 27, 1976, which were reflections on her life.

And bread lasts only a day;
But the touch of your hand
And the sound of your voice,
Sings on in the soul always.' "

"And now let us breathe a prayer of grateful memory for Lila W. Thompson: O God, before whom the generations rise and fall, And who gives to all one's task and mission, We praise You for the life and work of your servant, Lila, commemorated by a prayer-poem so appropriate to her spirit:

Lord, let me live from day to day
In such a self-forgetful way
That when I kneel to pray
My prayer shall be for others. Amen"[169]

As Rev. Perkins pointed out, she received many posthumous awards. She had secured passage of the bill to construct US Route 9 from Adelphia to Lakewood when she served in the Assembly. It had been named the John D. Rockefeller Highway. One of her greatest honors was when the NJ Legislature (at the beginning of the legislature's session, January, 1934) renamed it the Lila W. Thompson Memorial Highway and placed a large granite monument and plaque to this groundbreaker, now located beside US Route 9 at Adelphia Road, Route 524, Freehold Township, Monmouth County, "in tribute to and recognition of her unselfish and distinguished service to the State of New Jersey." It was the first highway dedicated to a woman in the USA; her keynote was service for the people. For more than thirty years (1934-1975) the Memorial had been located near Moroz Street in the Southard section of Howell Township on Route 9.[170]

---

[169] Perkins, Rev. F. Elwood Perkins, *Remarks* at the Re-dedication of Lila W. Thompson Memorial Monument, May 18, 1975
[170] *Asbury Park Press*, '77 Update, 1977. *NJ Assembly* and *Senate Resolutions* revisited this commemoration for the bicentennial, May 27,1976, Dad noted about the same time, a section of highway in Florida was named for a woman whose tomb was moved to build the highway.

Phillip Forman, Senior Judge, Third Circuit, U.S. Court of Appeals, Trenton, wrote to Claude for the May 1975 Commemoration: "I remember your mother well. She was dedicated to the principles of liberty upon which our Nation is founded and manifested her devotion to it in affirmative activity for the good of the people. This was demonstrated in the conduct of her office in the Assembly of the New Jersey Legislature and in the many other activities in which she engaged." [171] The Plumsted Township Bicentennial Commission Celebration honored New Egypt's First Citizen, Lila W. Thompson, with the above quote from Judge Forman and a recitation of some of her many accomplishments at the first Bicentennial event, a Sunday evening Band Concert May 16, 1976.[172]

In her reflections on the moral and religious significance of true servants of the people, Willa Cather paints her ideal pattern of morality and order: "Her heroine has a strong sense of morality, decorum, and what is proper: great sensitivity (which by itself, however, often leads to disaster), great strength and courage, an almost superhuman talent for heroic struggle and fortitude, most of all, a *faith* which is realized in the fertility rites of the seasons on the land, the sowing and the harvest, and in ceremonials (both secular customs and religious rituals), which are accepted without question or skepticism."[173]

Lila fit Willa Cather's description of the heroine and was indeed A *Woman For All Seasons!* Just imagine all she would have accomplished if she had lived longer.[174]

---

[171] Phillip Forman, U.S. Circuit Judge's *Letter*, May 14, 1975

[172] *NE Press*, May 13, 1976

[173] Hoffman, Frederick J., *The 1920's, American Writing in the Postwar Decade*, p.183

[174] Franklin D. Roosevelt became president exactly one month before Lila's death and began the changes in the economy that would end the Great Depression; the possibilities for Lila's contributions would have been unlimited.

Donald C. Thompson

EPILOGUE

"My sole defense, my only weapon, is a life of integrity, whether I meet honor or dishonor, praise or blame," is the verse that best affirms Lila's identity and actions, as well as her legacy.[175] As many have maintained, "In the final analysis, her legacy is in the hands of the people," for all ages.

POSTERITY

On Feb. 22, 1936, almost three years after Lila's death, a son was born in Charles Private Hospital, Trenton, to Irene and Claude Thompson, delivered by Dr. J. Edwin Obert: Donald Carlton Thompson, Lila and Joseph's only grandchild. I am a United Methodist minister, fulfilling Lila's prayer for Claude. I have four children: Joel adopted May 11, 1964 and born March 22, 1962; and three born to my former wife, Gail Yarbrough, and me: Tara Sunnarborg, born Dec. 6, 1962 and twins, Dale and Ross, born Aug. 5, 1964. At publication they have born Lila and Joseph's seven great-grandchildren, four girls: Lindsay, Taylor and Layne Thompson, and Amara Sunnarborg; and three boys: Lucas, Grayson and Cole Thompson. All reside in Florida, except for Joel in Arizona.

After 1933, Joseph spent the rest of his life as an Ocean County employee, mostly for the Board of Freeholders. He wrote materials for the board, such as his *Short Form Parliamentary Guide*, and did public relations for them. Joseph dated, but never re-married. He continued his lodge work and effective speaking throughout the state. He was closer to Sewell than to Claude. For example, for one year after Lila's death, Joseph and Sewell contested Lila's will

---

[175] II Corinthians 6: 3-4,7-10a, *The New Testament in Four Versions*: *J.B.Phillips Modern English*, Christianity Today, Washington, DC, 1965, p.559

deeding the funeral parlor to Claude.[176] Joseph died January 6, 1948, in his apartment in Beachwood, asphyxiated by his malfunctioning gas stove. The flame went out and because he apparently had been drinking, he did not detect the escaping gas. The New Egypt Methodist Church overflowed with mourners at his funeral. Sewell died January 29, 1958, apparently of a lung disease related to smoking.

Claude separated from Irene in early September 1954. Mother, apparently deeply distraught, committed suicide April 17, 1957. On September 4, 1957, Dad married Ruth Stahl Carson after relating to her for eight years. She was a Girard Trust Corn Exchange Bank vice-president, who trained many presidents and managers. Ruth assisted Dad in the annual commemorations of Lila at the US Route 9 monument, 1975-77. Claude had retired as a realtor in Island Heights, NJ. After Ruth's death due to an asthma attack, May 20, 1978, in their Frankfort, Philadelphia apartment, Claude returned to New Egypt to rent an apartment in the former Thompson homestead where he was born on 39 North Main Street and Lakewood Road. Although he wanted to die there, he spent his last years in the Masonic Home in Burlington where he died December 8, 1992, of intestinal complications. Joseph, Sewell, Carlton, Claude and Ruth are buried along with Lila in the Jacobstown School House Cemetery. Irene is buried with her parents and several sisters in the Odd Fellows Cemetery, Pemberton.

Claude and Irene Thompson cared for Lila's foster child, Wilbur R. Childers, from April 3, 1933 until after his high school graduation. After serving in the Merchant Marine in World War II, refueling tankers and administering medical care aboard ship, he spent most of his adult life living in Fanwood, NJ, working as a composer with Arrow Typography in Newark. He was a member of the Volunteer Fire Department and Rescue Squad in Fanwood. When Wilbur retired in 1990, he and his wife moved to Manchester, one mile from Lakehurst Naval Air Station. He spent his last six months

---

[176] *Last Will and Testament* of Lila W. Thompson to M. Claude Thompson, processed by court, Apr. 16, 1934

on the sickbed. He died September 13, 2001, of emphysema, ironically, at the Paul Kimball Medical Center in Lakewood, where Lila served on the board and tremendously aided the hospital in surviving during the Great Depression. The Fanwood Fire Department, in tribute to Wilbur and his lifelong service, paid all his funeral expenses. His wife, Mary (Mae), two daughters, Judith Kruze and Joyce Childers, two grandsons and five great grandchildren, survive Wilbur. What better tribute could he make to Lila than his life of service?[177]

My purpose in writing Lila's biography is to inspire persons to live lives of truth and integrity, no matter what the obstacles, and to aid those who are oppressed in life. People challenged by the witness of what she accomplished in her faith and life, are already pursuing their dreams in caring for all people. [178] Grandpa Joseph often told me one of their favorite stories: *The Little Engine That Could*, of a small railroad engine pulling the long heavy freight train up the steep incline, puffing, "I hope I can…I think I can…I know I can…I knew I could," in succession, as the engine made it to the top of the mountain and down the other side.

May your efforts contribute to harmony, democracy and peace on our planet.

---

[177] Jacobstown School House Cemetery, Pemberton Odd Fellows Cemetery; Claude Thompson's state certificate to care for Wilbur; Internet obituary information on Wilbur Childers found by Jane Thompson, and Mae Childers phone call, Oct. 1, 2002. I hadn't seen Uncle Wilbur Childers or his wife, Mae, and their daughters since they visited in my New Egypt home when I was a youngster. Over the years, we lost contact, until this and the previous phone call to their daughter, Judith.

[178] Response to my speeches and sermons on Lila, 2002, and conversation with Wilbur's daughter, Judith, August 18, 2002

From Proverbs 31 in the Hebrew Bible, these words signify the strength of character of fine women like Lila:

> A woman of valor—seek her out;
> She is to be valued above rubies.
> She opens her hand to those in need,
> And offers help to the poor.
> Adorned with strength and dignity,
> She looks to the future with cheerful trust.
> Her speech is wise and the law of kindness is on her lips.
> Those who love her rise up with praise and call her blessed.
> Many women have done well, but you, Lila, you surpass them
>   all.
> Charm is deceptive and beauty short lived,
> But a woman loyal to God has earned praise.
> Honor her for her work; her life proclaims praise.[179]

---

[179] Hebrew Bible version of Proverbs 31:10,20,25-26,28-31 from Rabbi Barbara Aiello, Temple Beth El, Bradenton, FL, Summer, 2002

BIBLIOGRAPHY

Aiello, Barbara, from a HEBREW BIBLE version, PROVERBS 31: 10,20,25-26,28-31, Summer, 2002

Goodman, Paul & Gatell, Frank O., USA AN AMERICAN RECORD, Dryden Press, Hinsdale, IL, 1972, Vol 2

Heston, Alfred M., ed., SOUTH JERSEY, A HISTORY 1664-1924, Lewis Historical Publications, NYC & Chicago, 1924, Vol. III

Heller, Milton F., Jr., THE PRESIDENTS' DOCTOR, AN INSIDERS VIEW OF THREE FIRST FAMILIES, Vantage Press, NYC, 2000

Hoffman, Frederick J., THE 20'S, AMERICAN WRITING IN THE POSTWAR DECADE, Macmillan Paperback, New York, 1965

Langer, William L., ed., AN ENCYCLOPEDIA OF WORLD HISTORY, Houghton Mifflin, Harvard, Cambridge, MA, 1952

Miller, Pauline S., OCEAN COUNTY, FOUR CENTURIES IN THE MAKING, Ocean County Cultural & Heritage Commission, Toms River, NJ, 2000

Mount, Dorothy S., A STORY OF NEW EGYPT AND PLUMSTED TOWNSHIP, Heidelberg Press, Burlington, NJ, 1979

Perkins, Rev. F. Elwood, REDEDICATION OF MEMORIAL MONUMENT OF LILA W. THOMPSON HIGHWAY, May 18, 1975 & May 27, 1976

Smith, Cynthia H., OCEAN COUNTY WOMEN IN THE LEGISLATURE: THE STRUGGLE FOR EQUALITY IN REPRESENTATION, Ocean County Cultural and Heritage Commission, 1998

Saunders, Ernest W., SEARCHING THE SCRIPTURES, A HISTORY OF BIBLICAL LITERATURE, 1880-1980, Scholars Press, Chico, CA, 1982

Seeger. Pete, writer; The Byrds rendition: TURN, TURN, TURN, lyrics to music from ECCLES1ASTES 3:1-8, 1960's

Thompson, Donald C., THE APPLICATION OF PAULO FREIRE'S APPROACH TO U.S. ADULT EDUCATION, California State University, Long Beach, 1977

Thompson, Donald C., MY AUTOBIOGRAPHY, Mrs. Elizabeth Kauffman's English Class, Allentown, NJ High School, 1950-51

Thompson, Joseph M. SHORT FORM PARLIAMENTARY GUIDE, Ocean County Board of Chosen Freeholders, Toms River, NJ, 1926

ASBURY PARK PRESS, Asbury Park, NJ, '77 Update, 1977; May 17, 1965, Nov. 4, 1996

ASSOCIATED PRESS release, Cassville, NJ, Apr. 4, 1933

AUTOGRAPH BOOK to Lila W. Thompson, Jan. 1886

BRADENTON HERALD, Bradenton, FL, Orlando, FL lynching article, Nov. 6, 2002

EXPLORING THE HISTORY OF SOUTHERN OCEAN COUNTY, pamphlet, Long Beach Island, NJ, 1979

FAMILY BIBLE of Lila W. Thompson, 1912, Family Records section

FRONTIER HOUSE, PBS-TV, Apr. 29-30, 2002

GENERAL ASSEMBLY AND SENATE OF NEW JERSEY RESOLUTIONS, Rededication of the Lila W. Thompson Highway, May 27, 1976

HANKINS FILE, Ocean County Historical Society, Toms River, NJ, 1998

HISTORY OF NEW EGYPT IN THE PINES, Moore Brothers, New Egypt, Ocean County, NJ, 1911

THE HOLY BIBLE, KING JAMES VERSION, Thomas Nelson Publishers, Nashville, TN, 1994

INTERVIEW of CHILDERS, MAE, by telephone by Donald C. Thompson, Oct. 1, 2002

INTERVIEW of LEAR, CAROLYN, by Donald C. & Jane R. Thompson, New Egypt Historical Society, June 26, 2002

INTERVIEWS of IVINS, MILDRED POTTER, by Donald C. & Jane R. Thompson, New Egypt, NJ, 1998, 1999, 2000, 2001, 2002

INTERVIEW of KRUZE, JUDITH CHILDERS, by telephone by Donald C. & Jane R. Thompson, Aug. 18, 2002

INTERVIEW of MORGAN, ELIZABETH MIERS, Forked River, NJ, by Donald C. & Jane R. Thompson, 1998

INTERVIEW of NORTON, ELEANOR HOLMES, Philadelphia, PA by Terry Gross, WHYY-FM Radio, Fresh Air, 2002.

INTERVIEWS of POTTER, KENNETH, by Donald C. & Jane R. Thompson, New Egypt, NJ, 1986, 1998, 1999, 2000, 2001, 2002

INTERVIEW of RYAN, ANN ROCKHILL, by Donald C. & Jane R. Thompson, New Egypt Historical Society, June 26, 2002

INTERVIEW of THOMPSON, M. CLAUDE, by Fote, Linda, New Egypt, NJ, for OCEAN COUNTY WOMEN: MAKERS OF HISTORY, National Organization of Women, Feb. 1983

INTERVIEWS of THOMPSON, M. CLAUDE, by Donald C. & Jane R. Thompson, New Egypt, & Burlington, NJ, 1951, 1976, 1978, 1985, 1986, 1989, 1992

THE JERUSALEM BIBLE, Doubleday, Garden City, NY, 1968

LAKEWOOD CITIZEN, Lakewood, NJ, June 5, 19, 26, 1925

LAKEWOOD FREE PRESS, Lakewood, NJ, Oct. 11, 25, 1923, May 22, 1958

LAST WILL AND TESTAMENT OF LILA W. THOMPSON to M. CLAUDE THOMPSON, from the court, Apr. 16, 1934

LETTER from FORMAN, PHILLIP, Senior Judge, Third Circuit, U.S. Court of Appeals to Thompson, M. Claude, May 14, 1975

LETTER from MACK, CONNIE, Owner-Manager, Philadelphia American Base Ball Club to Thompson, Sewell, Jan. 4, 1916 and subsequent LETTERS to and ARTICLES about Sewell, 1915, 1916

LETTER from PERKINS, REV. F. ELWOOD, Methodist Pastor in New Egypt, 1931-33, Oct. 18, 1977 and NOTES from Commemoration Presentations, May 1975, 1976, 1977 & 1979

LETTER from THOMPSON, M. CLAUDE to Thompson, Donald C., Nov. 2, 1977

MANUAL OF THE LEGISLATURE OF NEW JERSEY, 1924, 1925, 1930, 1931, Josephine A. Fitzgerald, Trenton, NJ

NEW EGYPT PRESS, New Egypt, NJ: Nov. 11; Dec. 9, 1906: Nov. 8, 1908: Sept. 8, 1911: Oct. 23; Dec. 18, 1914: July 8; Nov. 29 1920: Apr. 26; May 31; June 28; July 12; Aug. 2; Sept. 20, 27; Oct. 4, 11, 18, 25; Nov. 8, 15; Dec. 13, 20, 1923: Jan. 10; Feb. 5, 12, 19; Mar. 13, 20, 1924: Jan. 1; Feb. 19; Mar. 19; June 4, 18, 25, 1925: July 9, 30; Sept. 3, 1931: Apr. 14, 1932: Oct. 12,

1950: Mar. 11; Nov. 11, 1971: May 13; Dec. 2, 30, 1976: June 25; Dec. 1, 1977: May 15, 1980: May 28, 1986

NEW JERSEY COURIER, Toms River, NJ, Sept. 28; Oct. 12, 19, 26, 1923: June, 1925: May 22, 1958: June 20, 1974

NEW JERSEY LEGISLATIVE INDEX, 1925, Fitzgerald, in NJ Historical Library, Trenton, NJ, March 7, 1989

NEW JERSEY WOMEN IN THE LEGISLATURE, UNIQUE VOICES, UNIQUE SERVICE, Fitzgerald's NJ Legislative Manual, Sept. 12, 1995

NEW YORK CITY MAIN PUBLIC LIBRARY EXHIBIT. Dec. 2001

NEW YORK CITY METROPOLITAN MUSEUM OF ART SPECIAL EXHIBIT, Dec. 2001

THE NEW YORK TIMES, Oct. 23, 1915: Nov. 7, 1923

THE NEW TESTAMENT IN FOUR VERSIONS: KING JAMES, REVISED STANDARD, PHILLIPS MODERN ENGLISH, NEW ENGLISH BIBLE, Christianity Today, Washington, DC, 1965

OCEAN COUNTY BIRTH AND WEDDING RECORDS, 1850-1931, Elizabeth Ann Grant research, 1989

"ONE HUNDREDTH ANNIVERSARY OF THE METHODIST CHURCH BUILDING, NEW EGYPT, NJ," Anniversary Church Bulletin, 1951

PLUMSTED TOWNSHIP (USA) CENSUS, 1920, Elizabeth Ann Grant research, 1989

PLUMSTED TOWNSHIP BIRTH AND WEDDING RECORDS, 1850-1931, Elizabeth Ann Grant research, 1989

THE RISE AND FALL OF JIM CROW; THE TERRORS OF RACISM; Part 3, PBS-TV, Oct. 15, 2002

THOMPSON FAMILY ORIGIN and COAT OF ARMS

TRENTON EVENING TIMES, Oct. 11, 1950

TRENTON STATE CAPITOL TOUR, Sept. 2000, Jan. 2001

UCLA GRADUATE SCHOOL OF EDUCATION, History of Education Classes, Los Angeles, CA Sept.-Dec. 1972

WMNF-FM Radio, Tampa, FL Public Affairs Programming, Nov. 6, 2002

GLOSSARY

Assembly = General Assembly, together with the Senate, form the New Jersey Legislature

Co. = County

DAR = Daughters of the American Revolution, chronicling the colonies' militia & Continental Army & Navy

D of A = Daughters of America, a prominent national women's lodge in Lila's lifetime

DC = District of Columbia, including the city of Washington

GAR = Grand Army of the Republic; chronicling Civil War Union troops

Jan. = January. Jan. and other months are abbreviated in quotes.

Jr. = Junior, a male with the same name as senior

Jr. OUAM = Junior Order of United American Mechanics, a lodge/fraternal order

MA = State of Massachusetts and other states are indicated with US Postal abbreviations

NE = Town of New Egypt in Ocean County, New Jersey

NJ = State of New Jersey

OC = Ocean County, New Jersey

OES = Order of the Eastern Star, the women's lodge connected to the Masonic Lodge

PBS = Public Broadcasting System, television network

Rep. = Representative

RR = Railroad

3 R's = Reading, (w)riting, and (a)rithmetic; regarded then as the basic subjects in school

She = Where not otherwise designated, refers to Lila W. Thompson

Sr. = Senior, a man with the same name as junior

The Shore = New Jersey beaches and communities on the Atlantic Ocean

Suffrage = Women's right to vote granted August 26, 1920, in the Nineteenth Amendment to US Constitution

US or USA = United States of America

UT = United Transportation Company, the central New Jersey telegraph and railroad company headquartered in New Egypt

WWI = World War I, 1914-1918
WWII = World War II, 1939-1945
W. = Worrell: Lila's middle name or initial from another family's last
    name

TIME LINE

March 9, 1875 = Lila W. Robbins the twelfth of sixteen children was born of Theodore Robbins, Sr. and Lydia A. Hankins, of New Egypt, NJ

1881—1888 = Lila attended the one room red school house in Archertown

1888—early 1891 = Lila attended Professor Horner's Classical Academy in New Egypt

April 25, 1891 = Lila married Joseph M. Thompson of New Egypt in Asbury Park, NJ; managing his first successful campaign, Joseph becomes Chief Republican Page, US House of Representatives

October 25, 1893 = First child, a son, "Sewell" Murdock Thompson born. During early marriage, Lila also helped raise William Gibberson and Theodore Robbins, Jr's children

1898 = US intervened in Spanish-American War; Spain withdrew from Cuba, ceded Guam, Puerto Rico, and the Philippines to US, which becomes a world power

1899 = Thomas A. Mathis bought the first automobile, a Cadillac, in Ocean County

April 8, 1900 = Second child, a son, Joseph "Carlton" Thompson born

September 14, 1901 = President William McKinley, Republican, assassinated; Theodore Roosevelt, Republican, became US President; Joseph M. Thompson, Chief Republican Telegrapher & Page, US House of Representatives

1903 = Lila elected Associate National Councilor, D of A

August 12, 1905 = Third child, a son, Milton "Claude" Thompson born

November 5, 1906 = Mother, Lydia A. Robbins, died

1907-1908 = Thompsons live in Washington, DC; while Joseph served as Chief Telegrapher-Page, Republican

March 4, 1909 = William Howard Taft, Republican, became US President

August 7, 1909 = son, Carlton, died; shortly after his death, first automobile purchased by Thompsons, one of the first in New Egypt; soon Lila became State Councilor, D of A (twice)

1913 = Lila served as National Councilor, D of A

March 4, 1913 = Woodrow Wilson, Democrat, became US President

1914 = Lila joined OES in Lakewood; became State Chair & Secretary, Degree of Pocahontas

1915 = Lila founded New Egypt OES, began first term of two as NJ Grand Matron

October 22, 1915—1933 = Lila Director, D of A Orphans' Department

May 19, 1917 = Father Theodore Robbins, Sr. died

1914-1918 =WWI; 1917-18 = Sewell served in US Army, WWI after brief baseball career

1919 = Eighteenth Amendment, US Constitution, prohibiting alcoholic beverages passed

August 26, 1920 = Nineteenth Amendment, US Constitution adopted, granting women suffrage; Lila member NJ & officer, Ocean County Republican Committees

March 4, 1921= Warren Harding, Republican, became US President; died in office, August 2, 1923

September 1921 = Lila, first Ocean County woman to run for elective public office; Lila lost first campaign for Assembly

1922 = Lila officer NJ & Ocean County Republican Women's Clubs

August 2, 1923 = Calvin Coolidge, Republican, sworn in as US President, served through 1929

September 25, 1923 = Lila, first foreman (forewoman) of a US Grand Jury, won OC Republican Primary for NJ Assembly

November 6, 1923 = Lila won General Election for NJ Assembly, first woman representative of an entire county

January 8, 1924 = Lila began first of two terms in Assembly, under Governor Silzer

March 7, 1924 = Legislature passed Lila's first bill; Assembly Speaker appointed her to six committees, Chair of three.

Summer, 1924 = Lila receives foster son, Wilbur Childers; Lila selected first Chair OC Library Commission

November 4, 1924 = Lila re-elected to Assembly, under Republican Governor Edge

December 2, 1924 = Ocean County Free Library founded; Lila Chairs the first Library Commission and established libraries.

January 1925 Legislative Session began= Lila presented the Bill that was approved constructing/paving of Route 9, Adelphia to Lakewood, NJ. opening The Shore to resort development, tourism, etc.

June, 1925 = Lila lost bid for NJ Senate to Republican Party boss, Thomas A. Mathis

March 4, 1929 = Herbert Hoover, Republican, became US President

October 1929 = US Stock Market Crash; Great Depression began

January 1930 = Joseph M. Thompson began first of two terms in NJ Assembly

July 23, 1931 = M. Claude Thompson and Irene De Cou married

September 9, 1931 = Wilbur Childers entered Allentown NJ High School

April 1931 = Lila, first woman Chair of Board of Stewards, New Egypt Methodist Church

January 21, 1932 = Lila appointed first Director, OC Old Age Assistance (Welfare) Bureau

April 3, 1933 = Lila died an untimely death in single car crash, Cassville, NJ

June 1933 = Joseph lost NJ Senate race to Percy Camp, Tom Mathis' handpicked candidate

January 1934 = NJ Legislature Joint Resolution designated the Adelphia-Lakewood Road (Route 9) as Lila W. Thompson Memorial Highway, first US highway named for a woman

February 22, 1936 = Donald Carlton Thompson born to Claude & Irene Thompson, Lila & Joseph's only grandchild

1937-1976 = Kenneth Potter, Lila's nephew, member/Mayor, Plumsted Township Committee

January 7, 1948 = Joseph M. Thompson died in Beachwood, NJ, asphyxiated

May 18, 1958 = Thomas A. Mathis, party boss, committed suicide in the midst of scandal

1973 = Lydia A. Robbins Tripple, Lila's last sibling died in Ocean City, NJ

May 16, 1976 = Lila honored as New Egypt's First Citizen by Plumsted Township Bicentennial Commission; Lila honored 1975-77, 79 in Memorial Services at the Route 9 monument to Lila

Donald C. Thompson

State of New Jersey
(Seal)

GENERAL ASSEMBLY
STATE HOUSE, TRENTON, NJ

———————

ASSEMBLY RESOLUTION

By Assemblymen Newman and Doyle
Adopted May 27, 1976

———————

Whereas, On Sunday, May 23, 1976, memorial services paying tribute to the late Lila W. Thompson, a pioneer among women in public service in this State, were held at the monument on the Lila W. Thompson Memorial Highway (Adephia -Lakewood Road), Ocean County; and

Whereas, Mrs. Thompson, born Lila W. Robbins in New Egypt, was the first woman to represent a county in the General Assembly, serving as the sole member from Ocean county in the 1924 through 1925 Legislatures, when she was a member of six committees and chairman of three; and

Whereas, Married in 1891 to Joseph M. Thompson of New Egypt, who shared her active interest in political life, and who later also represented their county in the Assembly from 1929 through 1931. She was county Republican Vice Chairman in 1920 and State Committeewoman in 1921-22, and served for two years as a member of the Board of Governors of the New Jersey Republican Club; and

Whereas, She was a member and officer of numerous fraternal, civic and community organizations, and became the first Director of the Ocean County Welfare Board and the first Chairman of the Ocean County Library Commission; and

Whereas, in 1934, the year following her death the Legislature, by joint resolution, designated the Adelphia-Lakewood Road, the construction of which she had been instrumental in obtaining during her terms in the General Assembly, as the Lila W. Thompson Memorial Highway "in tribute to and recognition of her unselfish and distinguished service to the State of New Jersey;" now, therefore

Be It Resolved by the General Assembly of the State of New Jersey:

That this House hereby joins with the people of Ocean County in honoring the Memory of Lila W. Thompson, who was among the first and most prominent of the women of this State to play a distinguished role in the public life of the State and commends and concurs in the memorial tribute paid to her in the ceremonies held on May 23: and

Be It Further Resolved: That a duly authenticated copy of this resolution signed by the Speaker and attested by the Clerk, be transmitted to her son, M. Claude Thompson.

Signed: Joseph A. LeFante, Speaker; Attest: J. Miller, Jr., Clerk of the General Assembly

State of New Jersey
(Seal)

THE SENATE
STATE HOUSE, TRENTON, NJ

SENATE RESOLUTION

By Senator Russo
Adopted May 13, 1976

Whereas, On Sunday, May 23, 1976, memorial services paying tribute to the late Lila W. Thompson, a pioneer among women in public service in this State, will be held at the monument on the Lila W. Thompson Memorial Highway (Adephia - Lakewood Road), Ocean County; and,

Whereas, Mrs. Thompson, born Lila W. Robbins in New Egypt, was the first woman to represent a county in the General Assembly, serving as the sole member from Ocean county in the 1924 through 1925 Legislatures, when she was a member of six committees and chairman of three; and,

Whereas, Married in 1891 to Joseph M. Thompson of New Egypt, who shared her active interest in political life, and who later also represented their county in the Assembly from 1929 through 1931. She was county Republican Vice Chairman in 1920 and State Committeewoman in 1921-22, and served for two years as a member of the Board of Governors of the New Jersey Republican Club; and,

Whereas, She was a member and officer of numerous fraternal, civic and community organizations, and became the first Director of the Ocean County Welfare Board and the first Chairman of the Ocean County Library Commission; and,

121

Whereas, in 1934, the year following her death the Legislature, by joint resolution, designated the Adelphia-Lakewood Road, the construction of which she had been instrumental in obtaining during her terms in the General Assembly, as the Lila W. Thompson Memorial Highway "in tribute to and recognition of her unselfish and distinguished service to the State of New Jersey;" now, therefore,

Be It Resolved by the Senate of the State of New Jersey:
That this House hereby joins with the people of Ocean County in honoring the Memory of Lila W. Thompson, who was among the first and most prominent of the women of this State to play a distinguished role in the public life of the State and commends and concurs in the memorial tribute to be paid to her in the ceremonies which will be held on May 23: and,

Be It Further Resolved: That a duly authenticated copy of this resolution signed by the President and attested by the Secretary, be transmitted to her son, M. Claude Thompson.

Signed: Matthew Tillman, President; Attest: Robert E. Gladden, Secretary of the Senate

FAMILY TREE:
Descendants of Zacheriah HANKINS, SR.
Chart 1

1. Zacheriah HANKINS, SR. (b.1754 d.1850)
    sp: Phebe HERBERT (b.1761 d.1834)
    +-2. Zacheriah HANKINS, JR. (b.1780 d.1831)
        sp: Ann RIDGEWAY (b.1784)
        +-3. James Benson HANKINS (b.1807 d.1853)
            sp: Rejoice CHAMBERLAIN (b.1808 d.1830)
            +-4. Lydia A. HANKINS (b.1837-New Egypt, NJ or
                Burlington County, NJ d.5 Nov1906-New Egypt, NJ)
                sp: Theodore ROBBINS (b.1832-New Egypt, NJ d.19
                May1917-New Egypt, NJ)
                +- **5. Lila Worrell ROBBINS (b.9 Mar 1875-New
                Egypt, NJ d.3 Apr 1933-Lakewood Road,
                Cassville, NJ)**
                    sp: Joseph Murdock THOMPSON (b.17 Dec
                        1871-New Egypt, NJ m.25 Apr 1891 d.7 Jan
                        1948-Beachwood, NJ)
                    - 6. Sewell Murdock THOMPSON (b.25 Oct
                        1893-New Egypt, NJ d.29 Jan
                        1958-Vicentown, NJ)
                        sp: Ethel CHAFEY (m.7 Nov   1912)
                        sp:Marion MCGINLEY (m.31 Aug1919)
                        sp: Jennie TRIMMER (m. 29 Aug1931)
                    - 6. Joseph Carlton THOMPSON (b.8 Apr 1900
                        d.7 Aug 1909)
                    +- 6. Milton Claude THOMPSON (b.12 Aug
                        1905-New Egypt, NJ d.8 Dec 1992-
                        Burlington,.NJ)
                        sp: Irene DE COU (b.5 Nov
                            1906-Pemberton, NJ m.23 Jul 1931 d.17Apr
                            1957-New Egypt, NJ)
                            sp: Ruth STAHL (b.9Feb1916-
                                Wrightown,NJ m.4Sept1957 d.20May
                                1978-Phila.PA)

123

FAMILY TREE: Chart 2

+-7. Donald Carlton THOMPSON (b.22 Feb 1936-Trenton, NJ Charles Private Hospital)

    sp: Melba Gail YARBROUGH (b.20 Sep 1938-Virginia m.25 Nov 1960)

      sp: Jane RILEY (b.7 Jun 1936-Belle Plaine, IA m.6 Jun 1976)

- 8. Joel Kelley THOMPSON (b.22 Mar 1962-Oakland, CA)

- 8. Tara Denise THOMPSON (b.6 Dec 1962-Reno, NV, St. Mary's Hospital)

    sp: Duane Joseph SUNNARBORG (b.7 Mar 1963 m.21 Aug1993)

    +- 9. Amara Jane SUNNARBORG (b.28 May 1994-Sarasota, FL)

- 8. James Dale THOMPSON (b.5 Aug 1964-Reno, NV, St. Mary's Hospital)

    sp: Elizabeth MONT (b.13 May 1966 m.13 Aug1988)

    - 9. Lindsay Jean THOMPSON (b.15 Jan 1990-Bradenton, FL)

    - 9. Lucas James THOMPSON (b.4 Mar 1992-Bradenton, FL)

    +- 9. Layne Elizabeth THOMPSON (b.3 Dec 1997-Bradenton, FL)

- 8. Donald Ross THOMPSON (b.5 Aug 1964-Reno, NV St. Mary's Hospital)

    sp: Sharon BEBER (b.21 Feb 1965 m.31 Jan1987)

    - 9. Taylor Nicole THOMPSON (b.15 Jan 1994-Sarasota, FL)

    - 9. Grayson Ross THOMPSON (b.4 Mar 1997-Sarasota, FL)

FAMILY TREE:

Chart 3

+- 9. Jordan Cole THOMPSON
(b.26 Aug 1999-Sarasota, FL)

-5. Johnson ROBBINS (b.30 May 1855-New Egypt, NJ)
-5. Elmira ROBBINS (b.24 Dec 1856-New Egypt, NJ)
-5. Elmina ROBBINS (b.4 Jun 1859-New Egypt, NJ)
-5. John H. ROBBINS (b.28 Dec 1860-New Egypt, NJ d.CA)
-5. William ROBBINS (b.16 Dec 1862-New Egypt, NJ)
-5. Anna ROBBINS (b.5 Nov 1864-New Egypt, NJ)
-5. Charles ROBBINS (b.19 Sep 1866-New Egypt, NJ)
   sp: Carrie GLOVER
-5. Theodore ROBBINS, JR. (b.15 May 1868-New Egypt, NJ)
-5. Estella ROBBINS (b.1871-New Egypt, NJ d.5 Nov 1906)
   sp: George H. POTTER
-5. Samuel ROBBINS (b.16 Dec 1872-New Egypt, NJ)
   sp: Matilda BLUM
-5. Carrie ROBBINS (b.3 Mar 1873-New Egypt, NJ)
-5. Leon ROBBINS (b.25 Feb 1880-New Egypt, NJ)
-5. Lewis ROBBINS (b.25 Feb 1880-New Egypt, NJ)
-5. Lydia A, ROBBINS (b.28 Aug 1882-New Egypt, NJ d.1973-Ocean City, NJ)
   sp: George H. TRIPPLE (m.29 Nov 1900)
-5. Mary ROBBINS
   sp: Jake. MCKAIG

Donald C. Thompson

ABOUT THE AUTHOR

Author, Donald C. Thompson, photo by Neal France, Long Beach, CA

The author's education includes B.A., Dickinson College, Carlisle, PA; M. Div., Drew University, Madison, NJ; Ed.D., UCLA, Los Angeles; and Ph.D., Pacific Western University, Los Angeles. He is a retired United Methodist minister, university professor, public speaker, author, counselor and social activist. Don lives with his wife, Jane, in Bradenton, Florida, where they direct TRANSITIONS SUPPORT GROUP helping persons through life changes.

Printed in the United States
20442LVS00006B/301-552

9 781410 753205